# FAVORITES
## From The
# WORLD'S
# BEST CUISINES

*A World of Great Taste!*

by

Ela Kozak Küçükçakar

*"Favorites from the World's Best Cuisines"*

**Art director, decorator, food stylist and cook** : Ela Kozak Küçükçakar
**Recipes and Typography:** Ela Kozak Küçükçakar
**Photography:** Ela Kozak Küçükçakar and Kayhan Küçükçakar
**Cover Photo:** Herbed Ground Beef Stuffed Eggplants, "Karniyarik".

**Order Information:**

Ela Kozak Küçükçakar
P.O. Box 25152
Tempe, AZ 85285
U.S.A.

ISBN # 0-929526-70-8
Printed in the United States

**American Educational Press**
4123 North Longview
Phoenix, Arizona 85014
U.S.A.
(602) 274-7236

# A Culinary Adventure

My long and delightful culinary adventure started with my family in Ankara, then moved to Istanbul, Europe and the United States. During this time, I have had the opportunity to taste beautiful dishes prepared by famous Turkish, European and Asian chefs. On many special occasions, great presentations and food styling techniques that I have seen later became the pre-training part of my cooking adventure.

Growing up in a family who love to travel to exciting places, to try new tastes, to experience cultural diversities, and find the beauty in arts and music taught me to appreciate finer things in life. They greatly influenced me to explore and to learn more about people and their cultures.

My father loved to eat beautifully prepared meals, every dinner was another gourmet feast at home or dining out. The presentation of the meal was important to him as well as the taste. Being an architect, he always loved the beautiful. A romantic trip by gondola in Venice, Italian songs, beautiful Italian women, rhythm of colors, beautifully decorated meals and good taste, seafood dishes from Marmara and Aegean seas were his favorites.

My mother's travels to Europe started when she was a law student at the Ankara University. She is still traveling, seeing new places, sampling and cooking new and exciting dishes. She currently lives in Istanbul, Turkey. Eventough she has visited France so many times, if you ask her today, she still prefers Turkish and French cuisines; trips around Turkey and a trip back to Paris. She is totally in love with Istanbul and Paris. Her pleasures in Turkey include having a romantic dinner in Çiragan Palace by the Bosphorous, having a light afternoon tea in Sari kösk before the ballet in Atatürk Art and Culture Center, having böreks and enjoying laughter on the way to Emirgan, tasting the great selections in Beyti and Hasir gourmet kabob (kebab) restaurants, spending summers in beautiful Marmaris and Bodrum, inhaling the fresh scent of pine trees in Marmaris, swimming in crystal clear Aegean and Mediterranean seas, eating local fresh fruit and vegetables. In France, her delights include Châteaubriand or filet mignon with sweet currant sauce prepared with wine, having a sweet crêpes suzette on the way to Luxembourg park, a romantic evening in Trocadéro, watching artists at Montmartre, enjoying a coffee break at Sacré Cœur, an evening at lido in Champs-Elysées.

Three years ago, thanks to the positive reaction that I received for my cooking, I decided to gather this beautiful and delightful adventure into a cookbook. My travels in Turkey, Europe, The United States and exotic islands; many enjoyable tasting and cooking experiences from exquisite and authentic cuisines; beautiful presentations from famous chefs and great influence from my family all have helped me to create this book.

"Favorites from the World's Best Cuisines" includes my new recipes, reinterpreted classic and family recipes and ideas integrated from the recipes of the famous chefs. The recipes offer delicious and authentic Turkish dishes from the great Turkish cuisine for a rich and delightful feast, exquisite French dishes for special occasions, the dishes that you can enjoy taking a step back from the fast pace of life and a delightful selection from world cuisines. The amount of oil, butter, egg and certain vegetables such as onion and garlic are reduced for better and pleasant experiences.

My favorite recipe for culinary happiness is a blend of love, curiosity, patience and an attention to detail. Bon Appetite! Afiyet Olsun!

Ela Kozak Küçükçakar, 1997

# Turkish Cuisine

Ottoman chefs created delicious dishes for the sultans for centuries in culturally rich Middle East and left today's Turkey with an extraordinary culinary heritage. Some of today's popular dishes have their roots in recipes written 700 years ago. The Turkish cuisine is considered one of the top three world cuisines and offers a tremendous selection of authentic dishes.

These overwhelming variety of dishes, each with a unique combination of ingredients, a way of preparation and presentation can be categorized into: grilled meats, grain-based, vegetables, seafood, desserts and beverages. Before describing each of these categories, some general comments are necessary. Each category of dishes contains only one or two types of main ingredients. Turks are purists in their culinary tastes; the dishes are supposed to bring out the flavor of the main ingredients rather than hiding it behind sauces or spices. Thus, the eggplant should taste like eggplant, lamb like lamb, pumpkin like pumpkin. Contrary to the prevalent Western impression of Turkish food, spices and herbs are used with zucchini, parsley with eggplant, a few cloves of garlic has its place in some cold vegetables, cumin mixed in ground meat when making "köfte". Lemon and yogurt are used to complement both meat and vegetable dishes, to balance the taste of olive oil or meat. Most desserts and fruit dishes do not call for any spices. So the flavors are refined and subtle.

According to the historians Turks rolled their first börek and bread-type dough almost a millennium ago. Böreks are baked or fried variety of ways with using several types of dough (page 129 and 130). When you walk into specialty dessert and pastry shops "Baklavaci-Börekçi" in Turkey, you would find an extensive selection of these böreks as well as extensive selection of baklava type desserts. Börek is a special-occasion food which requires great skill and patience, unless you are able to buy thin sheets of dough already rolled out from your corner grocery store. Anyone who accomplish this delicate task using the rolling pin, becomes the most sought-out person in their circle of family and friends. The sheets are layered or folded into various shapes before being filled with cheese or meat mixes and baked or fried. Every household enjoys at least five different varieties of börek as a regular part of its menu.

There are more than 30 kinds of desserts made with sweet syrup using phyllo type dough, shredded dough (tel kadayif), and other types of dough (page 160 and 161). The most well known sweets associated with the Turkish Cuisine are the Turkish delight and the "Baklava", giving the impression that these are the typical desserts eaten after meals. This is not true. First, the family desserts is much richer than these two. Secondly, these are not typical desserts as part of a main meal. For example, baklava and its relatives are eaten usually with a coffee, as a snack or after a kabob dish.

Most wonderful contribution of the Turkish Cuisine to the family desserts, that can easily be missed by casual explorers, are the milk-based healthy desserts with unique tastes (page 162). These are "guilt-free" puddings made with starch and rice flour, and, originally without eggs or butter. In addition to this, There is a large selection of soft-gourmet candies made with pistachios and almond pastes, candies made with whole chestnut, chestnut pieces, chocolate and nuts "Sam fistigi ezmesi, badem ezmesi, kestane sekeri, çikolatali kestane sekeri" (page 173). Turkish delight (soft candies made from sugar or honey topped with coconut flakes and nuts) are part of the sweets in Turkish cuisine that can be found at baklavaci-börekçi (dessert and pastry shops) and sekerci (gourmet candy stores).In addition, you can find other types of desserts (including western interpretations) at pastahane (cake and dessert shops in Turkey.

Kabob "Kebap" is another category of food which, like the börek, is typically Turkish dating back to the times when the nomadic Turks learned to grill and roast their meat over their camp fires. Given the numerous types of kebabs, it helps to realize that you categorize them by the way of the meat is cooked. Restaurants which specialize in kebaps generally have an extensive selection of kebaps (over 20 kinds). Meat grilling techniques are much the same around the world, but nowhere are they better used than in Turkey, justifiably famous for its shish kabob (Sis kebap-page 73). Sis kebap is grilled cubes of skewered meat. Döner kebap is made by stacking alternating layers of ground meat and sliced leg of lamb on a large upright skewer, which is slowly rotated in front of a vertical grill. As the outer layer of the meat is roasted, thin slices are shaved and served. There are numerous other grilled kebaps beside those cooked in a clay oven. It should be noted that the unique taste of kebaps are due more to the breeds of sheep and cattle, which are raised in open pastures by loving shepherds, than to special marinades and a way of cooking. "Izgara", mixed grilled meat is how main course meat dishes are prepared at a kebab restaurant. Mixed grills are likely to include lamb chops, köfte and sis. The way of preparing ground meat will be the "köfte" (page 69). These are grilled, fried, oven-cooked or boiled, after being mixed with special spices, eggs, and grated onions and carefully shaped into balls, oblongs, round or long patties.

Turkish cuisine has a large selection of vegetable dishes. Vegetables are also consumed in large quantities in the Turkish diet. The simplest and most basic type of vegetable dish is prepared by slicing a main vegetable such as zucchini or eggplant, combining it with tomatoes, green peppers and onions, and cooking slowly in butter and its own juices. Since the vegetables that are cultivated in Turkey are truly delicious, a simple dish like this, eaten with a sizeable chunk of fresh bread, is a satisfying meal for many people.

Cooking with olive oil is one of the fine and healthy ways to cook vegetables (page 55, 56 and 59). The vegetables and the oil work beautifully together, each bringing out the taste of the other. These dishes are refreshing, soft textured, healthy and not at all greasy. A whole class of vegetables is cooked in olive oil. Practically all vegetables such as fresh string beans, artichokes, root celery, leek, eggplants, pinto beans, or zucchini can be cooked in olive oil, and are typically eaten at room-temperature. So they are a staple part of the menu with variations depending on the season.

Then, there are the fried vegetables such as eggplant, peppers or zucchinis that are eaten with a tomato or a yogurt sauce (page 57). Yogurt, a contribution from Turks to the world, has also become a popular health food. A staple in Turkish diet, it has been known all along for its detoxifying properties.

"Dolma" is the generic term for stuffed vegetables, being a derivative of the verb "doldurmak" or to fill; it actually means "stuffed" in Turkish. There are two categories of dolmas: those filled with a meat mix or with a rice mix. The latter are cooked in olive oil and eaten at room- temperature (page 58). The meat dolma is a main-course dish eaten with a yogurt sauce, and a very frequent one in the average household (page 70). Any vegetable which can be filled with or wrapped around these mixes can be used in a dolma, including zucchini, eggplants, tomatoes, cabbage, and grapewine leaves. However, the green pepper dolma with the rice stuffing, has to be the queen of all dolmas, a royal feast to the eye and the palate. In addition to these general categories, there are numerous meat and vegetable dishes which feature unique recipes. The eggplant (or aubergine) has a special place in the Turkish cuisine. According to the Turkish cooks, there are 60 ways to prepare an eggplant dish. This handsome vegetable with its brown-greencap, velvet purple, firm and slim body, has a richer flavor than that of its relatives found elsewhere. At a party, a frustrating question to ask a Turk would be "How do you usually cook your eggplant?", a proper answer to this question would require hours! Here, it will have to suffice to mention two eggplant dishes that are a must to taste. In one, the egg plant is split lengthwise and filled with a meat mix "Karniyarik" (page 63). This is a common summer dish, eaten with rice pilaf. The other one is "Her Majesty's Favorite", a delicate formal dish that is not easy to make but well worth trying. The name refers to Empress Eugenie, the wife of Napoleon III, who fell in love with it on her visit to Sultan Abdulaziz. The name of the dish is also being used as "Sultan's Favorite" (page 77).

Four seas (the Black Sea, the Marmara Sea, the Aegean and the Mediterranean) that surround the Turkland are rich in seafood and residents of the coastal cities are experts in preparing their fish. Winter is the premium season for eating fish. That is the time when many species of fish migrate from Black sea to warmer waters and when most fish reach their mature sizes. So, the lack of summer vegetables is compensated by the abundance of fish at this time. Every month has its own preferred fish along with certain vegetables which complement the taste. The local seafood of Marmara and Aegean seas such as fishes: levrek, barbunya, karagöz, trança; shelled seafood: prawn and lobster are delicious and their tastes are unique to the region. Seafood dishes are cooked in several special ways which would also seal the flavor inside them.

If you plan to visit to Turkey do not forget to visit locals' favorite dessert and pastry shops, restaurants which specialize in authentic Ottoman/Turkish cuisine and kebaps. Also, do not forget to taste the famous KahramanMaras ice cream that is made with new age interpretation, offering variety of flavors.

Have a wonderful adventure, taste the most delicious cuisine, see the rich history and the culture, the beautiful nature; and meet the friendly people.

# Acknowledgments

I would like to thank my mother, Leman, for encouraging me to write this book and for giving me the opportunities and encouragement to explore the beautiful and good things in life.

I would like to thank my husband, Kayhan, for his support, for his publishing efforts and for taking the photographs.

I also thank my sister, Deniz, for her support and for sharing her professional experience.

Without my loved ones Leman, Deniz, Kayhan this book would never have been published.

I would also like to express my appreciation to the Turkish Ministry of Foreign Affairs for providing me with background information about Turkish cuisine.

# DEDICATION

To my mother and father

**LEMAN and OKTAY KOZAK**

For the beautiful, For the best

# Contents

**Lentil Soup, page 3**

**Creamy Mushroom Soup, page 4**

**Herbed Cheese Ball, page 9**

**Guacamole Arizona, page 9**

**Scallops from St. Croix, page 15**

**Deluxe Omelette, page 21**

**Artichoke Salad, page 28**

**Chicken with Spinach, page 36**

**Chicken Portugal with Mushroom Sauce, page 39**

**Circassian Chicken, page 40**

**Chicken Cordon Bleu, page 44**

**Vegetable Garnished Artichokes, page 55**

**Stuffed Grape Leaves, page 58**

**Pinto Beans Cooked with Olive Oil, page 59**

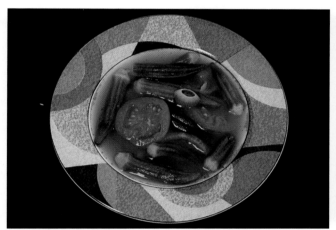

**Okra Stew, page 60**

**Filet Mignon with Mustard Caper Sauce, page 63**

**Herbed Ground Beef Stuffed Eggplants, page 63**

**Châteaubriand, page 65**

**Beef Stew with Vegatables, page 66**

**Tenderloin with Peppercorn Sauce, page 68**

**Sultan's Favorite, page 77**

**Navarin of Lamb, page 81**

**Salmon Steaks at the Oceanview, page 94**

**Fish Fillets in Havarti Sauce, page 97**

**Oven-Baked Shrimp with Cheese, page 99**

**Rice Pilaf with Raisins and Almonds, page 112**

**Pan-Roasted Potatoes, page 117**

**Manicotti, page 121**

**Kiymali Börek (Turkish Pastry), page 130**

**Braid, page 132**

**Dinner Rolls, page 133**

**Cheese Almond Bread, page 134**

**Profiteroles, page 139**

**Deluxe Raisin Cake, page 141**

**Deluxe Almond Cake, page 142**

**Banana Cream Pie, page 146**

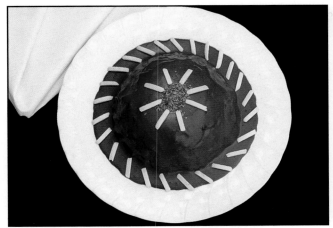

**Rich Chestnut-Chocolate Dome, page 150**

**Banana Roll Cake, page 152**

**Eclair, page 152**

**Blueberry Chese cake, page 153**

**Crème Caramel, page 154**

**Pistachio Christmas Ribbons, page 166**

**Rich Chocolate-Walnut Clusters, page 168**

**Almond Cookies, page 171**

**Pineapple Fruit Bowl, page 173**

**Ice cream with Morello-Cherry Sauce, page 174**

**Ela after a culinary work session**

**Fresh Crabs at Fisherman's Wharf, San Francisco**

# SOUPS

## Chicken Vegetable Soup

7 cups hot water
1 cup chicken broth
  or 1 chicken-flavor bouillon cube
1-1/2 chicken breasts cut into cubes
1 cup sliced carrots
1 cup peas
1 cup potatoes cut into cubes
1/4 teaspoon pepper
1/2 teaspoon mixed spices
  (tableblend)

1/2 small onion, chopped
1/2 teaspoon salt
1 tablespoon all purpose flour
1 egg yolk
2 tablespoons milk
2 tablespoons margarine

In large saucepot, over high heat, sauté onion with 1/2 tablespoon margarine until onions are translucent; add chicken, water, chicken broth, carrots, peas, potatoes and salt Bring to a boil. Reduce heat to low and simmer 20 minutes or until chicken is fork-tender.

Meanwhile, in medium bowl combine flour, egg yolk, salt, and remaining softened 1-1/2 tablespoons margarine and milk. Stir with fork to make a moist mixture. Stir this mixture into the soup and add pepper and mixed spices. Over medium heat, cook 20 minutes more. Serves 6.

## Lentil Soup

-Turkish-
6 cups hot water
1 cup beef broth (optional)
1 pound lentils
1 tablespoon shredded onion
1 lemon
Water to cover lentils

1 teaspoon salt
1/8 teaspoon pepper
1-1/2 tablespoons margarine
1-1/2 teaspoons tomato paste

In medium saucepan, over medium heat, heat lentils and water. Cook until lentils are tender. Remove from heat; drain lentils in colander. Grind lentils in covered food processor until desired smoothness; stir in 1 cup water and set aside.

In large saucepan in hot margarine, over medium heat, cook shredded onion until onion is tender. Add tomato paste and cook for 2 minutes. Add remaining 5 cups water or (4 cups water and 1 cup beef broth), diluted lentils, salt and pepper; stirring constantly. Cook for 30 minutes or until mixture gets thickened. Serve with lemon juice. Serves 4.

# French Onion Soup

*-French-*
*3 large onions, sliced*
*1 teaspoon sugar*
*1 tablespoon all-purpose flour*
*2-1/2 cups water*
*1/4 cup butter or margarine*

*1/2 cup red cooking wine*
*2 (10-1/2-ounce) cans condensed*
*  beef broth*
*1/2 cup shredded Swiss cheese*

In medium saucepan over medium heat, in hot butter, cook onions and sugar for 10 minutes. Stir in flour until well blended with the onions and pan juice.

Add water, wine and undiluted beef broth; heat to boiling. Reduce heat to low; cover and simmer 10 minutes. Ladle soup into serving cups and garnish with shredded Swiss cheese. Serve with French bread. Serves 4.


# Creamy Mushroom Soup

*-French-*
*1 pound mushrooms*
*1/2 cup butter or margarine*
*1 teaspoon lemon juice*
*1 small onion, sliced*
*1/3 cup all-purpose flour*
*3-1/2 cups water*

*3 chicken-flavor bouillon*
*  cubes*
*1 teaspoon salt*
*1/4 teaspoon pepper*
*1/2 cup heavy or whipping*
*  cream*

Trim tough stem ends of mushrooms; remove stems; set aside. Slice mushroom caps thinly. In 4-quart saucepan over medium-high heat, in hot butter or margarine, cook sliced mushrooms with lemon juice, stirring until mushrooms are just tender.

Reduce heat to medium-low. With slotted spoon, remove mushrooms to small bowl. Cook onion and stems in remaining butter; until onion is tender.

Stir in flour until blended; cook 1 minute, stirring the mixture constantly. Gradually stir in water and bouillon; cook stirring constantly until mixture is thickened.

Into blender container, ladle half of mixture; cover and at high speed, blend until smooth. Repeat with other half.

Return mixture to saucepan; stir in salt, pepper, cream and mushroom slices. Reheat until soup is just boiling. Serves 6-8.

# Broccoli Cheese Soup

*-American-*
1/4 cup butter or margarine
1/2 small onion, chopped
1/4 cup all-purpose flour
3 cups chopped broccoli
Water to cover broccoli

1/2 pound cheddar cheese, shredded
  (about 2 cups)
3 cups milk
2 cups chicken broth
1/2 teaspoon salt
Black pepper to taste

Prepare broccoli by removing any large leaves. Cut off any woody stalk ends; split stalks length wise to speed cooking.

In small saucepan over high heat, boil water and salt. Cook broccoli and salt 10 minutes until tender crisp. Drain; cut broccoli into flowerets; set aside.

In medium saucepan, over medium-high heat, in hot butter or margarine, cook onion until tender, about 5 minutes. Stir in flour and cook until flour has blended with onion.

Add chicken broth gradually; cook, stirring constantly, until mixture slightly thickened. Add milk, black pepper and heat just to boiling, stirring constantly. Add broccoli, over medium heat, heat just to boiling; remove from heat.

With wire whisk or slotted spoon, stir in cheese until melted. If cheese does not melt completely, cook over very low heat about 1 minute, stirring the soup constantly. Serves 4-6.

# Tomato Soup

*-Turkish-*
8 cups beef broth or
  hot water
1-1/2 tablespoons margarine
1 teaspoon all-purpose flour
1/2 teaspoon salt
1/2 teaspoon pepper

4 large tomatoes
1/2 small onion, shredded
1/2 cup shredded Swiss cheese
  (gruyère)
1/2 teaspoon sugar
Cream cheese (optional)

In large saucepan, cook onion until tender; add peeled, unseeded, chopped tomatoes and flour. Stir tomato mixture until flour is well blended.

Stir beef broth, sugar, salt and pepper into the tomato mixture; heat to boiling. Remove from heat, add cheese; stirring continuously. Before serving, if you like, drop 1/4 teaspoon cream cheese into bottom of each soup bowl. Serves 6-8.

# Beef Vegetable Soup

1/3 cup salad oil
1 small onion, diced
6 cups hot water
3 medium carrots, sliced
1 medium zucchini, cut
   into 1/2-inch cubes
1-1/2 pounds beef for stew,
   cut into 1/2-inch chunks
5 medium potatoes, cut into
   1/2-inch cubes

1 medium potato, shredded
1 (28-ounce) can tomatoes
1 (16-ounce) package cut green beans,
1/2 (8-ounce) can baby lima beans,
   drained
1/2 (8-ounce) can large kidney beans
1/2 teaspoons salt
1/2 teaspoon pepper
1/2 teaspoon basil

In large saucepot over high heat, in very hot salad oil, cook onion, carrots, green beans, cooked baby lima beans, cooked large kidney beans and zucchini until lightly browned, stirring frequently. With slotted spoon, remove vegetables to medium bowl; set aside.

In the same saucepot over high heat, in remaining oil, cook beef chunks, stirring frequently, until meat is well browned on all sides.

Meanwhile, peel potatoes; shred 1 potato and cut remaining 4 potatoes into 1-inch cubes. Add mixed vegetables, potatoes, tomatoes and remaining ingredients to cooked beef chunks; heat to boiling. Reduce heat to low; cover and simmer 25 to 30 minutes or just until beef chunks and potatoes are fork-tender. Serves 8-10.

# APPETIZERS

# Herbed Cheese Ball with Almonds and Gourmet Cheese Slices

1 (8-ounce) cream cheese
1/2 teaspoon minced garlic
1/2 teaspoon mixed spices
1/2 tablespoon finely minced
fresh parsley

roquefort, gruyère, baby Swiss, and
cheddar cheese slices
3 to 4 kinds of crackers
Whole almonds

Mix cream cheese, garlic, mixed spices and parsley and make a cheese ball. Place almonds over the cheese, oval sides up. Place the cheese ball onto cheese plate; arrange cheese slices and crackers around the cheese ball. Garnish with parsley. Serves 6-8.

# Sausage Snack Wraps

2 loaves of prepared frozen
bread dough
1 tablespoon tomato paste
1 teaspoon thyme
1/2 teaspoon chopped parsley
1/2 teaspoon onion powder
1/4 teaspoon garlic powder

3 tablespoons finely grated
parmesan cheese
1 teaspoon mixed spices
1/8 teaspoon salt
1 tablespoon margarine
1 tablespoon water if necessary
30 small party sausages

Thaw 2 loaves of dough. Separate each dough into 4 pieces. Unroll dough pieces into 1/2-inch thick rectangles. Cut 1-1/2x3-inch slices. In small bowl, mix rest of the ingredients except sausages. Brush dough slices with tomato paste mixture. Place sausages on one side of the dough slices, roll up to opposite point. Bake on ungreased cookie sheets for 20 to 30 minutes. Serves 15-20.

# Guacamole Arizona with Tortilla Chips

-Mexican-
2 avocado, finely chopped
1 teaspoon Grey Poupon mustard
Tortilla chips
1 teaspoon lemon juice

2 cups ready salsa
1 medium tomatoes, chopped
1 garlic clove, finely minced

In large bowl, mix chopped avocado, mustard, salsa, minced garlic, lemon juice and chopped tomatoes. Spoon mixture into medium serving bowl; set the bowl filled with guacamole on serving plate; surround with tortilla chips. Serve with your favorite beer. Serves 6-8.

## Turkey in Champagne Sauce with Toasted Bread Slices

1 tablespoon salad oil
2 (2-pounds) turkey breasts
4 cups water
1 medium onion, thinly sliced
1-1/4 teaspoon salt
1/2 teaspoon pepper
1/3 cup all-purpose flour

1-1/2 cups half and half
3 tablespoons butter or margarine
1/2 pound mushrooms, sliced
1 split dry champagne (about 6-ounces)
1/3 cup minced parsley
Toasted party bread slices

In large skillet over medium high heat, in hot salad oil, cook turkey breasts until well browned on all sides. Add water, onion salt and pepper; heat to boiling. Reduce heat to low; cover and simmer 1-1/2 hours or until turkey is fork-tender. Remove turkey from skillet; cool slightly until easy to handle. Cut turkey meat into 1-inch pieces; discard skin and bones. Meanwhile, over high heat, cook turkey broth in skillet until it reduces to about 1-1/2 cups.

In small bowl with spoon, blend flour with 1/2 cup half-and-half; gradually stir into broth until smooth; stir remaining half-and-half. Cook, stirring, until cream sauce boils and is thickened.

In medium skillet over medium heat, in hot butter or margarine, cook mushrooms until tender; gently stir into cream sauce with turkey meat, champagne and 1/4 cup parsley; heat. Serve with toasted party bread slices. Serves 6-8.

## Ham and Cheese Rolls

1 (1-pound) loaf prepared frozen
    bread dough from (3 pound) package
8 thin slices of ham

1 cup shredded cheddar or
    Swiss cheese
Sesame seeds

Preheat oven to 375 °F. Thaw 1 loaf. Unroll dough into 4 long rectangles. Place two slices ham on each rectangle; sprinkle with cheese. Starting with the shortest side, roll up each rectangle and press edges to seal. Coat rolls with sesame seed. Cut each of the 4 rolls into 5 slices. Place each slice seamside down on ungreased cookie sheet. Bake for 15 to 20 minutes or until golden brown. Immediately remove from the cookie sheet. Serve warm. Serves 4.

## Picadillo Filling with Tortilla Chips

-Mexican-

1/4 cup dried raisins, chopped
1/3 cup finely chopped onion
1 tablespoon vegetable oil
1/2 cup canned green chiles,
  finely chopped
2 tablespoons vinegar
Small taco shells and tortilla chips
1-1/2 cups grated cheddar cheese
1-1/2 cups chopped green onions
1-1/2 cups chopped tomatoes
1-1/2 cups Guacamole
1 cup shredded lettuce
Sour cream

1 tablespoon salt
1/8 tablespoon pepper
1 pound ground chuck beef
1 can tomatoes, chopped
1/3 cup pine nuts or silvered
  almonds

In large skillet, sauté onion in oil until translucent. Add green chiles, 1 tablespoon vinegar, salt and pepper. Add beef and raisins. Mix thoroughly until light brown, breaking up meat as it cooks. Add tomatoes and remaining 1 tablespoon vinegar. Bring to boil, then simmer until thickened (about 15 minutes). Stir in nuts, if desired. Makes about 3-1/4 cups. Place Picadillo in the center of the serving plate, arrange tortilla chips around it. Keep serving plate warm. Serve with small taco shells, grated cheddar cheese, green onions, chopped fresh tomatoes, Guacamole and sour cream. Serves to: 8-12

## Nachos from Laguna Beach

-Mexican-

1 can (16-ounce) refried beans
3/4 cup ready salsa
8-ounce (2 cups) shredded
  Monterey jack cheese

Pickled jalapeno slices, if desired
1 cup ground beef, sautéed in chopped
  onion
1 package tortilla chips

Combine beans, cooked ground beef and salsa; mix well. Arrange tortilla chips in a single layer on large microwave-safe platter. Spread 1/2 of bean mixture on chips. Top with 1 cup cheese and desired amount of jalapeno slices. Microwave on high for 1-1/2 to 3-1/2 minutes or until cheese is melted, rotating the plate 1/4 turn halfway through cooking. Repeat with remaining ingredients. Serves 6.

# Chile

*-Mexican-*
*1/4 cup vegetable oil*
*2 onions, chopped*
*2 cloves garlic, minced*
*2 pounds ground beef*
*1 can (12-ounce) tomatoes,*
*  semi-drained*
*1 can (11-ounce) red kidney*
*  beans, semi-drained*
*1/2 cup green pepper, chunked*
*1/4 cup chopped parsley*

*3 tablespoons chili powder*
*1 tablespoon tomato paste*
*2 teaspoons salt*
*1 teaspoon red cayenne pepper*
*1 teaspoon cumin powder*
*1 teaspoon marjoram leaves, crushed*
*1 teaspoon dried oregano leaves, crushed*
*Cheddar cheese, grated*

In large saucepot, heat oil. Add half of chopped onions and garlic; sauté until translucent. Add meat; cook until brown. Add remaining ingredients except cheese; mix well. Bring to boil. Reduce heat and simmer, partially covered, for 45 minutes. If you need add water. To serve, top with cheese and remaining onions. Serves to: 6

# Pepper Dip with Vegetables

*1 cup mayonnaise*
*2 tablespoons grated onion*
*2 teaspoons tarragon vinegar*
*2 teaspoons chopped chives*
*2 teaspoons chili sauce*

*1/2 teaspoon curry powder*
*1/2 teaspoon salt*
*1/4 teaspoon pepper*
*1/8 teaspoon ground thyme*
*Sliced fresh vegetables (carrots,*
*  zucchinis, cucumbers, etc.)*

In small bowl, stir all ingredients except vegetables; cover; refrigerate. Spoon into bowl; set on plate; surround with vegetables. Makes 1-2/3 cups dip.

# Salami Rolls

*1 (12 oz.) package*
*  sliced salami*
*30 cheddar cheese cubes stuffed,*
*  ripe green olives*

*Wooden picks*

Cut salami slices in half. Fold them in half one more time. Place olive in salami, roll over olive and secure with wooden pick. Serve with cheese and cracker plate. Serves to: 10

## Hot Artichoke Dip

1 can (14-ounces) artichoke
  hearts, drained, chopped
1 cup Italian salad dressing
1 cup (4-ounces) grated
  parmesan cheese

1 garlic clove, minced
Green onions, sliced and
  tomato, chopped for
  garnishing (optional)
Tortilla chips or crackers

Heat oven to 350 °F. Mix first 4 ingredients; spoon into 9-inch pie plate. Bake 20 to 25 minutes or until lightly browned. Sprinkle with sliced green onions and chopped tomato, if desired. Serve with tortilla chips or crackers. Makes 2 cups

## Garlic and Carrot Dip

-Turkish-
1-1/2 cups plain yogurt
1/4 cup sour cream
1/4 cup fresh dill, minced
1 cup carrots, shredded

3 garlic cloves, minced
Salt to taste
1 tablespoon olive oil
Toasted party bread or crackers

In medium bowl, mix yogurt, sour cream, minced dill, garlic, salt, olive oil and shredded carrots. If you like, sprinkle olive oil on top. Serve with toasted party bread or crackers. Serves 6.

## Stuffed Mushrooms

-Turkish-
1-1/2 pounds medium-large
  mushrooms
1/2 pound ground beef
1/2 cup Swiss cheese,
  shredded

1/4 cup seasoned bread crumbs
1 teaspoon mixed spices
1/4 cup parsley
Salt to taste
1 teaspoon onion powder

Remove stems from mushrooms; chop stems. Set mushrooms and stems aside. In large skillet, over medium heat, cook ground beef, parsley, salt, onion powder, mixed spices, until ground beef is thoroughly cooked. Remove from heat; spoon off all but 2 tablespoons drippings from skillet. In hot drippings over medium heat, cook mushroom stems until tender, about ten minutes, stirring frequently. Remove skillet from heat; stir in ground beef mixture, cheese and crumbs. Preheat oven to 450 °F. Fill mushroom caps with ground beef mixture. Place stuffed mushrooms in large jelly roll pan. Bake 15 minutes. In last 3 minutes, sprinkle shredded cheese over the stuffed mushrooms. Serves 15.

## Spinach Pâté

-French-

3 (10-ounce) packages frozen
  chopped spinach, thawed
1/4 cup butter or margarine
1 bunch green onions, thinly
  sliced
2 large carrots, coarsely shredded
1 cup half-and-half

1-1/4 teaspoons salt
1 teaspoon basil
1/8 teaspoon cayenne pepper
4 eggs
Watercress sprigs and carrot slices
  cut in mini flower shaped pieces

Place spinach in colander in sink; using back of wooden spoon, press spinach to remove moisture. With hands, squeeze spinach to remove any remaining moisture. With knife, finely chop spinach.

Grease well medium loaf pan; line bottom of pan with foil. In medium saucepan over medium heat, in hot butter or margarine, cook onions and carrots until tender, about 5 minutes, stirring frequently. Stir in spinach, half-and-half, salt, basil and cayenne pepper; heat to boiling. Remove saucepan from heat; stir in eggs. Spoon mixture into loaf pan. Spreading evenly; cover with foil. Place loaf pan in larger baking pan. Fill baking pan, with hot water to come 1-inch up sides of loaf pan. Bake in 375 °F oven for 1-1/4 hours or until knife inserted in center through foil comes out clean. Cool in pan on wire rack 15 minutes. Place 2 heavy cans on top to weigh down pâté. Refrigerate overnight. About 15 minutes before serving; remove cans and foil from top of pâté. With metal spatula, loosen pâté from pan. Invert platter over pan; then invert platter and pan together and lift pan off. Remove foil; cut pâté into slices. Garnish platter with watercress or carrot flowers. Serves 10.

## Yogurt with Cucumbers-Cacik

-Turkish-

6 cups plain yogurt
2 cups diced small cucumbers
Olive oil
Salt to taste

2 tablespoons fresh dill,
  minced
Water

In large bowl, stir yogurt, fresh cucumbers (not pickled), dill weed, salt to taste. Add 3-1/2 cups of water or the amount of water that gives the desired consistency, stir well. Sprinkle olive oil and dill on top. Serve during lunch or dinner in small cups. Serves 4-6.

## Scallops from St. Croix

1 pound fresh or thawed
  frozen bay scallops
3/4 cup water
2 tablespoons dry white wine
1/4 teaspoon salt
1/8 teaspoon cayenne pepper
2 tablespoons butter or
1/2 garlic clove, minced

1/2 pound mushrooms, sliced
1 small onion, minced
1 tablespoon chopped parsley
1/4 cup all-purpose flour
3/4 cup buttered crumbs
2 tablespoons grated parmesan
  cheese

In large skillet over high heat, heat to boiling scallops, water, wine, salt and cayenne pepper. Reduce heat to medium; simmer scallops 2 minutes or until tender. Drain scallops, reserving liquid; set aside. Grease 8 scallop shells or ramekings. Meanwhile, preheat oven to 400 °F. In the same skillet over medium heat, in hot butter, cook mushrooms and onion 5 minutes or until tender. Stir in garlic, parsley and flour. Gradually stir in reserved liquid and cook, stirring constantly, until mixture is thickened. Add cooked scallops to skillet and stir into hot thickened mixture. Carefully spoon the scallop mixture into greased shells or ramekings. Arrange shells in jelly-roll pan for easier handling. Sprinkle scallop mixture with buttered crumbs and cheese and bake 10 minutes or until crumbs are golden. Serve immediately. Serves to: 8

## Party Pizzas

2 loaves of prepared frozenbread
  dough from (3-pound) package
1(16 oz.) package hot dogs, sliced
5 tablespoons tomato paste
8 tablespoons shredded jack
  cheese
3 tablespoons margarine, melted
Water

1 teaspoon dried oregano
1 teaspoon mixed spices
1/4 teaspoon sugar
1/8 to1/4 teaspoon garlic powder
1/8 to 1/4 teaspoon onion powder
1/8 teaspoon salt (optional)
All-purpose flour

Thaw 2 loaves ready dough. In medium bowl, mix 3 tablespoons melted margarine, tomato paste, oregano, garlic, onion, salt and sugar. Add water to make a heavy sauce.

On floured surface, cut each dough loaf into 4 pieces, roll each dough pieces into 1/4-inch thick small pizza dough. Spoon the tomato paste sauce on pizza dough, top with sliced hot dogs and shredded jack cheese. If you like, brush edges with melted margarine. Place pizzas on floured baking pan. Bake in 350°F oven for 30 minutes or until crusts are golden. Serve with fruit juice. Serves 4.

## Pan-Fried Mussels with Garlic Dip-Sarimsak Soslu Midye Tava

-Turkish-

| | |
|---|---|
| 1 pint shucked mussels | 3 tablespoons butter or margarine |
| 2/3 teaspoon finely crushed saltines | 3 tablespoons salad oil |
| Lemon slices for garnish | Bread crumbs |
| 1 cup beer | All purpose flour |
| 1/2 cup water | |

*Garlic Dip:*

| | |
|---|---|
| Bread crumbs | Water |
| 2 to 3 garlic cloves, minced | Salad oil |
| 2 tablespoons sour cream | Salt and pepper to taste |

Clean mussels, place them in medium bowl filled with beer and water. Let the mussels marinate for 30 minutes. Drain mussels; pat them dry with paper towels. On waxed paper, sprinkle half of crushed saltines, place mussels on it. Pour beer and water into medium bowl, add 1 egg into the mixture, beat it, then cover mussels first with flour then egg-beer mixture and crumbs. Sprinkle the mussels with remaining crushed saltines. Make certain that the mussels are thoroughly coated with crumbs before frying them. In large skillet over medium heat, in hot oil, fry half of mussels, turning once, 5 minutes or until golden brown. Repeat. Serve with lemon slices and garlic dip.

Garlic Dip: In small bowl, mix sour cream, garlic, pepper, salad oil, water and salt. Mix all ingredients well, serve with fried mussels. Serves 6.

## Oysters with Parmesan Cheese from Long Beach

| | |
|---|---|
| 3 tablespoons butter or margarine | 1/8 teaspoon cayenne pepper or anisette |
| 1/2 (10-ounce) package frozen chopped spinach, slightly thawed | 1/4 cup dried bread crumbs |
| 1 tablespoon minced onion | 18 large oysters on the half shell |
| 1 tablespoon parsley, chopped | Parmesan cheese, grated |
| 1 bay leaf | Lemon wedges for garnish |
| 1/4 teaspoon salt | |

Preheat oven to 425 °F. In 1-quart covered saucepan over medium heat, in melted butter, cook spinach, onion, parsley, bay leaf, salt and cayenne, stirring occasionally, until spinach is heated through. Toss in bread crumbs; set aside. Place oysters in baking pan and spoon on spinach mixture. Sprinkle with cheese. Bake 10 minutes. Garnish with lemon. Serve with oyster forks. Serves 6.

# EGGS and OMELETTES

# Poached Eggs

Eggs may be poached in a variety of simmering liquids including water, milk, soup, tomato juice, vegetable cocktail juice and broth.

Lightly grease saucepan or deep skillet, pour in 1-1/2 inches water; over high heat, heat to boiling and reduce the heat to low, simmering. Break the egg into saucer and gently slip into the simmering water. Repeat with other eggs; cook 3 to 5 minutes until of desired firmness. Remove the cooked eggs from the liquid with slotted spoon. Drain eggs in spoon thoroughly over paper towels and serve at once.

# Eggs Benedict

*Hollandaise Sauce*
*4 eggs*
*2 English Muffins*

*Butter or margarine*
*4 slices cooked ham*

*Hollandaise Sauce:*
*3 egg yolks*
*2 tablespoons lemon*
*  juice*

*1/2 cup butter*
*  or margarine*
*1/4 teaspoon salt*

Hollandaise Sauce: Add egg yolks and lemon juice to double-boiler top; with wire whisk or slotted spoon, beat until well mixed. Place double-boiler top over bottom containing hot, not boiling water. Add one third of butter or margarine to egg yolk mixture and cook, beating constantly, until the butter is completely melted. Add another third of butter, beating constantly; repeat with remaining third, beating until mixture thickens and is heated through. Remove from heat; stir in salt. Keep warm.

Eggs Benedict: Poach 4 eggs until of desired doneness. Keep eggs warm. Preheat broiler. Split muffins; spread each half lightly with butter or margarine. Place, buttered side up, on broiling pan, with cooked ham alongside. Broil until muffin halves are toasted and ham is heated through. On heated platter, place ham slice on each muffin half; top each with poached egg. Generously spoon Hollandaise sauce over eggs. Serves to: 4

## Eggs Mornay

2 tablespoons butter
  or margarine
2 tablespoons all-purpose flour
1 teaspoon salt
1/2 teaspoon dry mustard
1/8 teaspoon pepper

Dash of hot pepper sauce
2 cups milk
1/4 cup grated parmesan cheese
8 eggs

In medium saucepan over medium heat, into hot butter or margarine, stir flour, salt, mustard, pepper and hot pepper sauce. Gradually stir in milk; cook, stirring constantly, until mixture thickened. Stir in cheese until melted. Preheat oven to 400 °F.

Pour half of sauce into 4 buttered 10-ounce custard cups or individual baking dishes. Break 2 eggs into each dish over sauce; spoon remaining sauce over eggs, leaving yolks partially uncovered. Bake eggs 15 minutes, or until of desired doneness. Serves 4.

## Mexican Omelette

*-Mexican-*
*4 eggs*
*1 small tomato, diced*
*1/4 small onion, chopped*
*2 tablespoons diced green
  bell peppers*
*1/2 cup shredded Monterey jack
  cheese*

*Salt to taste*
*1/8 teaspoon cayenne pepper*
*1/2 teaspoon mixed Mexican
  spices*
*Margarine or butter*
*1 tablespoon water*

Break the eggs into small bowl. Add salt, pepper, mixed spices and water. Beat the eggs vigorously with wire whisk or fork just enough to mix the egg yolks and whites. In omelette pan or skillet over medium heat, melt butter or margarine; tilt skillet so that the butter coats the entire surface of the pan. Pour in eggs all at once. Let them set around edge. Shake pan occasionally to keep omelette moving freely over the bottom of the pan. With metal spatula lift edge as it sets, tilting skillet to allow uncooked egg mixture to run under omelette. Continue to shake the pan for a few seconds longer until you can feel omelette sliding freely over pan surface. When omelette is set but still moist on surface, spoon vegetables and cheese on the half of the omelette and using spatula, lift the edge of omelette and quickly fold in half. Cover and cook for a few minutes. Slide omelette onto warm plate, garnish as you desire. Serves 2-4.

## Deluxe Omelette

5 eggs
2 tablespoons chopped
  tomatoes
1 tablespoon diced green
  and red bell peppers
1/4 cup sliced mushrooms

1 tablespoon water
Butter or margarine
2 cheddar cheese slices
1/4 cup diced ham
1/4 teaspoon mixed spices

Prepare eggs and cook as on page 20. Spoon vegetables, ham, and shredded cheese on half of the omelette, sprinkle mixed spices, using spatula lift the edge of the omelette and quickly fold in half. Cook for few minutes; lay out sliced 1x3-inch cheese slices over the omelette. Cover wait 2 minutes to melt cheese slices. Serves 2-4.

## la vache qui rit Omelette

4 eggs
3 la vache qui rit cheese
  wedges (French cheese)
1 teaspoon mixed spices
1 teaspoon onion powder

1/4 teaspoon garlic powder
1/2 tablespoon dried parsley
Butter or margarine
Salt
1 tablespoon water

In small bowl, mix la vache qui rit (the laughing cow) cheese, onion and garlic powder, parsley, mixed spices and salt to taste. In medium bowl, beat eggs; add la vache qui rit mixture; mix it well. In medium omelette pan over medium-low heat, in hot butter or margarine, pour la vache qui rit-egg mixture. Cover and cook until omelette is done. Turn omelette onto warm plate. Serves to: 2-4

## Grilled Tortillas with White Cheese and Tomato

4 large tortillas
1/4 pound Turkish white
  (feta) cheese
1/2 teaspoon onion powder

2 tablespoons minced fresh parsley
1/2 teaspoon mixed spices
1 large tomato, peeled and diced
Butter or margarine

In medium bowl, mix white cheese, onion powder, parsley, mixed spices. Add diced tomato, 1/2 tablespoon margarine. Mix it well. In large skillet over medium heat, melt butter or margarine; tilt skillet so that the butter coats entire surface of pan. Place one tortilla in pan; spoon white cheese mixture on half of the tortilla, using spatula lift the edge of the tortilla and quickly fold. When one side is golden turn the other side and grill until slightly golden. Repeat with remaining ingredients. Serve hot. Serves 2-4.

# SALADS

## Turkish Bean Salad-Piyaz

*-Turkish-*
*1 (16-ounce) package*
  *Great Northern beans*
*1 medium onion, sliced*
*1 large tomato*
*2 hard-cooked eggs, sliced*
*1/4 teaspoon white pepper*

*1/2 cup olive oil*
*3 tablespoons red wine vinegar*
*1 tablespoon salt*
*1/3 cup chopped parsley*
*Turkish olives or pitted ripe olives*

Rinse and sort beans in large saucepot. Cover with 2-inch hot water; bring to rapid boil; boil for 2 minutes. Remove from heat. Cover and let stand 1 hour. Drain and rinse.

In the same large saucepot over high heat, heat water, salt and beans to boiling. Reduce heat to low; cover and simmer beans 1 to 1-1/2 hours or until tender, stirring occasionally. Drain beans.

In large bowl, combine beans and red wine vinegar and set aside. Meanwhile combine sliced onion and salt; peel tomato and chop into small pieces. Add salted onion and chopped tomatoes, and olive oil to beans; garnish with olives and sliced eggs. Serves 8-10.

## Mediterranean Salad

*1/2 medium head iceberg*
  *lettuce*
*2 medium tomatoes*
*3 pickling cucumbers*
*1/2 small red onion*
*10 to 12 marinated Turkish*
  *olives for garnishing*
*1/4 cup grated parmesan cheese*

*2 tablespoons minced parsley*
*1/4 teaspoon minced mint (dried*
  *or fresh)*
*1/4 teaspoon black pepper*
*3 tablespoons red wine vinegar*
*1/2 cup olive oil*

Into large salad bowl, tear iceberg lettuce into bite-size pieces. Peel and slice the cucumbers and red onion; cut tomatoes into cubes. Add cucumbers, tomatoes and red onion to lettuce. Sprinkle with parmesan cheese. In small cup combine olive oil and remaining ingredients; pour over salad, toss to mix well; garnish with olives. Serve with garlic bread.

Garlic bread: Sprinkle olive oil, parmesan cheese, salt, mixed spices, oregano, parsley on bread slices, toast them. Serves 6-8.

## Turkish Eggplant Salad

-Turkish-

3 slim Mediterranean eggplants
  (6 to 8-inches long) or 8 Japanese
  eggplants
2 to 3 dollops of plain yogurt
1-1/2 tablespoons shredded onion
2 tablespoons minced parsley

1 tablespoon sliced green slim
  Anaheim pepper (optional)
1 teaspoon chopped onion
1/4 cup olive oil
Half lemon
3 small garlic cloves, minced
Salt

Rinse and dry eggplants; grill them on charcoal fire, or under the broiler or in the oven in large pan. With a tong, over medium heat, grill all sides until eggplants are soft inside.

With sharp knife, remove the softened and browned skin of eggplants, rest of the browned skin pieces can be removed easily, under running cold water. In blender container at low speed, blend cooked eggplants. Add onion and minced garlic. Stir in olive oil, lemon juice, yogurt, salt to taste and parsley. Spoon eggplant mixture onto medium platter, garnish with diced peppers and parsley leaves. Eggplant salad can be served as an appetizer. Serves 6-8.

## Chicken Salad

1 head leaf lettuce
1/2 pound fresh mushrooms
4 tomatoes
1 medium cucumber
4 small chicken breasts, grilled
1/4 cup walnuts or pecans
1 bunch parsley or watercress

3 tablespoons mayonnaise
1 tablespoon dry mustard
2 tablespoons chutney
4-6 tablespoons sour cream
Salt and pepper to taste

Rinse lettuce; drain well. Tear into small pieces. Clean and slice mushrooms. Rinse tomatoes and cucumber.

Cut chicken meat into small bite-size pieces. Cut tomatoes into wedges. Peel and slice cucumber. Chop nuts coarsely.

Combine all ingredients in large salad bowl. Garnish with watercress or parsley. For dressing, blend mayonnaise and mustard. Add chutney and sour cream and stir. Season with salt and pepper. Serve dressing alongside. If you like serve with hot rolls or French bread and white or rose wine. Serves 4.

# Pasta Salad

1-2/3 cups spiral pasta, cooked
2 cups vegetables broccoli florets
 cherry tomatoes, sliced ripe
 olives, mushrooms, zucchini,
 chopped carrots and green
 onions

3 tablespoons prepared pesto sauce
3 tablespoons red wine vinegar
1/2 teaspoon pepper
1 cup julienned cooked turkey
3/4 cup cottage cheese
Water

In large bowl, combine pasta, vegetables and turkey. In food processor or blender puree remaining ingredients; pour over pasta mixture. Toss to coat thoroughly. Serves 4.


# Italian Salad

-Italian-
1 (8-ounce) package ham
2 medium potatoes
3 to 4 dill pickles
Water

1/2 pound cooked veal tongue
7 tablespoons mayonnaise
1/2 teaspoon salt

In medium saucepan over high heat, heat potatoes and water to boiling. Reduce heat to low; cover; simmer 20 to 30 minutes until potatoes are fork tender.

Drain potatoes and allow to cool slightly. Into medium bowl, with sharp knife, peel and dice potatoes. Slice pickles; dice ham and veal tongue, (reserve some for garnishing), mix with potatoes; add salt and mayonnaise, mix well. Spoon onto serving plate, garnish with ham, veal tongue and pickle slices. Serves 4-6.

## Artichoke Salad

2 (9-ounce) packages
  frozen artichoke hearts
3/4 cup olive oil or
  salad oil
1/2 cup lemon juice
1 tablespoon sugar
1 teaspoon Grey Poupon mustard

1-1/4 teaspoons salt
1/2 teaspoon pepper
1/2 teaspoon basil
1 pound mushrooms, sliced
1 tablespoon diced red pepper
1 small garlic clove, crushed
Water

In small saucepan, over high heat, heat artichokes in water for 2 minutes; drain them thoroughly. In small blender, blend olive oil, salt, sugar, mustard, pepper, basil and garlic. Stir this crisp mixture in artichoke hearts, sliced mushrooms and diced red pepper. Serves to:4

## Winter Salad

-Turkish-
1 head leaf lettuce
2 carrots, shredded
1/2 medium head red cabbage
2 tablespoons finely chopped
  fresh parsley

4 red radishes
1/4 cup olive oil
1/4 cup lemon juice
1/2 teaspoon salt

Rinse lettuce leaves and red radishes thoroughly, drain in colander. In large salad bowl, tear lettuce into bite-size pieces; slice radishes; slice red cabbage; add shredded carrot and parsley. In small cup, mix olive oil, lemon juice and salt. Pour over salad; toss it well. Serves 6-8.

## Coleslaw

1/2 cup mayonnaise
1 tablespoon milk
1 tablespoon lemon juice
1/2 teaspoon sugar
1/4 teaspoon salt
1/8 teaspoon paprika
1/8 teaspoon pepper

1 medium head cabbage
1 celery stalk
1 large carrot
1 tablespoon minced onion

Dressing: In small cup, with wire whisk, stir mayonnaise, milk, lemon juice, sugar, salt, paprika, pepper until well blended, set aside.

With sharp knife, shred cabbage; cut celery stalk into small pieces; with grater shred carrot. In large salad bowl, toss all ingredients with dressing. Serves 6-8.

## Beet Salad

*-Turkish-*
*1 large potato, cooked, peeled and cut into 1/2-inch cubes*
*2 (14-1/2 oz.) cans whole pickled beets, diced*
*4 tablespoons mayonnaise*

*1/4 cups pickled sweet jalapenos, sliced*
*2 dill pickles*

Cut cooked potato into 1/2-inch thick cubes. Drain beets; combine them with sliced sweet peppers and potatoes in medium bowl; stir in mayonnaise. Garnish with sliced dill cucumbers.

If pickled beets are not available. Substitute regular canned beets and prepare as follows. In small cup combine salt and vinegar to taste and 1/8 teaspoon minced garlic with beet juice. Dice whole beets into l/2-inch cubes; add diced beets into juice; mix and let stand for 30 minutes. Serves 6.


## Potato Salad

*6 medium potatoes*
*Water*
*1 medium red onion or 3 to 4 green onion, finely chopped*
*1/2 teaspoon pepper*
*1/2 teaspoon salt*

*1/2 teaspoon Grey Poupon mustard*
*3 tablespoons mayonnaise*
*2 tablespoons minced parsley*
*1 lemon, juiced*

In large saucepan over high heat, heat potatoes and water to boiling. Reduce heat to low; cover and simmer until they are fork-tender.

Drain potatoes and allow to cool completely; peel with sharp knife. In large salad bowl dice potatoes, add finely chopped green onions, salt, lemon juice and pepper; toss it. In small cup, mix mayonnaise and mustard and stir in salad, mix thoroughly. Serves 6-8.

## Tuna Salad

2 (7-ounce) cans tuna
1-1/2 cups sliced celery
1/2 cup chopped California walnuts
Lettuce leaves

1/4 cup sliced stuffed olives
1/4 cup French dressing
1/4 cup mayonnaise
1 teaspoon minced onion

French Dressing:
3/4 cup olive oil or
  salad oil
1/4 cup wine vinegar

1/2 teaspoon salt
1/8 teaspoon pepper

Combine all ingredients in large bowl, except lettuce leaves; toss to mix well; cover with plastic wrap and refrigerate. Serve on lettuce leaves.

French Dressing: Into small bowl or covered jar, measure all ingredients; stir with fork or cover and shake until thoroughly mixed. Cover and chill. Stir or shake the dressing just before serving. Serves 4.

## Deluxe Seafood Salad

1-1/4 cups mayonnaise
1 (2-oz.) can flat anchovies,
  drained, finely chopped
2 tablespoons tarragon vinegar
  or white-vine vinegar
2 tablespoons finely chopped
  parsley
2 tablespoons sliced chives
  or green onion tops
1 small garlic clove, minced

3/4 teaspoon finely chopped tarragon
3 qts torn romaine lettuce or
  combination of romaine and iceberg
  lettuce
1 pound medium shrimp, crabmeat or
  lobster, cooked, shelled
1 avocado, sliced
12 cherry tomatoes or tomato wedges
12 ripe olives

In small bowl, combine mayonnaise, anchovies, vinegar, parsley, green-onion tops, garlic and tarragon. Cover refrigerate a few hours to let flavors blend.

In large bowl, toss half of the mayonnaise mixture with lettuce. Divide lettuce mixture among 6 plates. Spoon shrimp, crabmeat or lobster evenly over lettuce mixture. Garnish each with avocado, tomatoes and olives. Pass remaining dressing separately. Serves 6.

## Shrimp Salad

3 cups shrimp, cooked,
1/4 cup sliced stuffed olives
1/2 cup sliced celery
1/2 cup chopped green bell pepper
1/2 cup chopped California
  walnuts

1/4 cup mayonnaise
1 teaspoon onion, minced
Lettuce leaves
French dressing

French Dressing:
3/4 cup olive or salad oil
1/4 cup wine vinegar
1/2 teaspoon salt
1/8 teaspoon pepper

In large salad bowl, combine all ingredients except lettuce leaves; toss well; cover with plastic wrap and refrigerate. Serve on lettuce leaves.

French dressing: In small bowl, with fork, stir olive oil, wine vinegar, salt and pepper. Cover and chill; stir well before serving. Serves 4.


## Classic Crab Louis

1 pound cooked fresh or
  frozen Alaskan King crab
1 cup mayonnaise
3 tablespoons chopped green
  onion
1 tablespoon Worcestershire
1 tablespoon red wine vinegar
1 teaspoon ketchup

Lettuce leaves
3 hard-cooked eggs, sliced
1 cucumber, sliced
1 tomato, sliced
1/2 teaspoon salt
1/8 teaspoon white pepper
2 teaspoons lemon juice

In medium salad bowl, mix mayonnaise, ketchup, Worcestershire, red wine vinegar, lemon juice, onion, salt and pepper; refrigerate for 1/2 hour. In salad platter, first make large encircled rings with lettuce leaves, egg, cucumber and tomato slices, heap crab in center; spoon half of the dressing over crab meat. Serve remaining dressing separately. Serves 4.

# POULTRY

## Stuffed Mediterranean Chicken

4 whole boneless chicken breasts
1 cup shredded Swiss or parmesan
   cheese
1/2 small onion, shredded
1 cup sliced mushrooms
1/4 cup olive or salad oil

1/4 cup minced parsley
2 tablespoons mixed spices
1 teaspoon salt
1 teaspoon garlic powder or
   1 garlic clove, minced
6 tablespoons margarine
4 tablespoons all purpose flour

In small bowl, mix shredded cheese, shredded onion, sliced mushrooms, olive oil, parsley, mixed spices, salt and garlic. With meat mallet pound each chicken breast until 1/4-inch thick.

With spoon, spread the stuffing to within 1/2-inch of edges. Fold chicken breasts over filling. Carefully roll in flour and place in freezer open end down until firm, 5 to 10 minutes.

In large skillet, over medium-high heat, in hot margarine, arrange stuffed chicken breasts, open end down. Cook seam sides first and continue cooking until browned on all sides and tender.

Serve with potatoes au gratin or rice pilaf with vegetables. If you like, fasten edges with wooden picks before arranging chicken breasts. Serves 4.

## Chicken with Rosemary

-Turkish-

4 whole boneless chicken breasts,
   cut into 1-inch cubes
2 potatoes, cut into 1-inch cubes
2 carrots peeled, sliced 1/4-inch
   pieces
1 cup peas
2 cups sliced mushrooms

1/2 cup butter or margarine, melted
1 cup water
1/4 teaspoon pepper
1/2 teaspoon salt
2 teaspoons dried rosemary

In large oven pan, combine chicken, potatoes, carrots, peas, mushrooms, pepper, salt, water, margarine. Sprinkle rosemary over the chicken-vegetable mixture. Cover with aluminium foil and cook in 350 °F oven approximately 45 minutes or until vegetables and chicken are tender. Remove foil during last 10 minutes. Serves 4.

# Chicken with Spinach

-Turkish-

4 whole boneless chicken breasts
1/2 (10-oz.) package spinach,
  thawed, chopped
1/2 small onion, chopped
3 teaspoons mixed spices
1/2 teaspoon black pepper
1 teaspoon salt
1/4 teaspoon red pepper

4 Swiss or Turkish casserie cheese slices
4 tablespoons margarine
1/2 cup dry white wine
1 chicken-flavor bouillon cube
1 tablespoon all-purpose flour
1 cup whipping cream
Salt to taste
3 tablespoons water

Two years after creating this recipe for my family. I read in a Turkish newspaper that a Turkish chef won an international culinary award for his similar recipe, using spinach as a filling. Trying to eat more vegetables and make a good balance between meat and vegetables helped me to create this recipe.

In medium saucepan over medium heat, in 2 tablespoons hot margarine, cook onion until tender; add spinach, mixed spices (tableblend), red and black pepper and salt; cook for 15 to 20 minutes.

With meat mallet, pound each chicken breast until 1/4-inch thick. Place Swiss cheese slices on chicken fillets. Spread spinach filling to within 1/2-inch from the edges. Fold chicken breasts over the filling. Place in freezer, open end down until firm, 5 to 10 minutes.

In large skillet over medium heat, in hot margarine; cook chicken breasts open end down first then cook until golden on all sides. Add 1/4 cup wine; reduce heat to low; cover and simmer 20 minutes.

Meanwhile, in small saucepan over medium heat, cook 3 tablespoons water, 1/4 cup white wine, bouillon, flour, whipping cream and salt to taste until mixture has slightly thickened.

Pour thickened sauce over chicken breasts; simmer 10 minutes more. Serves 4.

# Herb-Roasted Chicken

1 (6-pound) whole chicken
1/4 cup salt
1 teaspoon parsley flakes
3/4 teaspoon thyme leaves

1/2 teaspoon sage
1/8 teaspoon cracked pepper
Salad oil

Remove giblets and neck from inside bird. Rinse bird under running cold water and drain well. Place in roasting pan breast side up, lift wings up toward neck, then fold under back of bird to balance it. Mix salt and next 4 ingredients and rub over out side and in body cavity. Cover and refrigerate at least 12 hours or overnight. Brush skin with oil and roast, uncovered, in 325 °F oven 3 to 4 hours, basting frequently. Serves 8.

## Chicken in Spicy Sauce

*-Italian-*
*1 (3-pound) chicken, cut up*
*1 (16-ounce) can tomatoes*
*12 small white onions, peeled*
*2 large green peppers, cut into*
*strips*
*1 tablespoon salad oil*
*1/2 cup dry red wine*

*1-1/2 teaspoons garlic salt*
*3/4 teaspoon basil*
*1/4 teaspoon pepper*
*2 tablespoons all-purpose flour*
*2 tablespoons water*

In large skillet over medium-high heat, in hot salad oil, cook chicken pieces until golden on all sides.

Stir in tomatoes with the liquid, wine, garlic salt, basil and pepper; heat to boiling. Reduce heat to low; cover and simmer 15 minutes. Add onions and green peppers; cover and simmer just until vegetables are fork-tender.

In cup, stir all-purpose flour and water until smooth; stir into chicken mixture and cook, stirring frequently, until mixture is boiling and thickened. Serves 4.

## Brandied Chicken with Artichoke Hearts

*3 large boneless chicken breasts,*
*halved*
*All-purpose flour*
*2 tablespoons salad oil*
*2 tablespoons margarine*
*3/4 tablespoon salt*
*1/8 teaspoon white pepper*

*1-1/2 cups water*
*2 chicken-flavor bouillon cubes*
*1 cup sour cream*
*1 (9-ounce) packages frozen*
*artichoke hearts, thawed and drained*
*3 tablespoons brandy*
*2 teaspoons lemon juice*

On waxed paper, dust chicken breasts with 1/4 cup flour. In large skillet over medium-high heat, in hot salad oil, cook chicken until lightly golden on all sides. Place chicken in large baking dish; set aside. Preheat oven to 350 °F.

In small saucepan over low heat, in melted margarine, stir 2 tablespoons flour with salt and pepper until smooth. Gradually stir in brandy, lemon juice, water, chicken bouillon and cook, stirring constantly, until thickened and smooth. With wire whisk, gradually blend in sour cream; pour mixture over chicken.

Cover baking dish tightly with foil and bake chicken 45 minutes. Remove foil from baking dish and add artichoke hearts; cook until artichoke hearts are tender. Serves 6.

## Walnut and Carrot Stuffed Chicken

3/4 cup coarsely ground
  walnuts
6 medium boneless chicken breasts,
  cut in half
1 to 2 carrots, peeled and shredded
1/4 cup minced parsley
1/2 teaspoon red pepper

1-1/4 cups milk
2 tablespoons all-purpose flour
1 chicken-flavor bouillon cube
Parsley for garnish
Butter or margarine
1 teaspoon salt

In small bowl, combine walnut, shredded carrot, minced parsley, 1/2 teaspoon salt, 2 tablespoons melted butter or margarine; set aside. With meat mallet pound each chicken piece until 1/4-inch thick.

To stuff the chicken breasts, overlap two pieces about 1-inch; spread walnut mixture to within 1/2-inch of edges; fold two long sides slightly toward middle; roll chicken breasts upward; if you like fasten open ends with two wooden picks. Repeat this process with remaining of the chicken pieces.

In small cup, stir in melted 1/2 cup butter or margarine, salt and red pepper until well mixed. Arrange stuffed chicken breasts, open side down in large baking dish. Pour melted butter mixture over the chickens; brush chickens with butter mixture. In 400 °F oven, bake 40 minutes or until chicken is fork-tender, basting occasionally with pan drippings. If you like serve with gravy.

Gravy: Spoon 3 tablespoons pan drippings into small saucepan, over medium heat, stir flour, bouillon and 1/2 teaspoon salt until blended. Gradually stir in milk; cook, stirring constantly, until mixture is thickened.

Discard wooden picks, arrange stuffed chicken breasts on warm platter, garnish with chopped parsley, serve with gravy. Serves 6.


## Chicken Marinated in Chili

1 (12-ounce) bottle chili sauce
1/2 cup red wine vinegar
1 tablespoon horseradish

1 garlic clove, quartered
3/4 teaspoon salt
1 (3-pound) broiler-fryer, cut up

In medium baking dish, mix all ingredients except chicken to make a marinade. Place chicken in marinade; cover and refrigerate chicken at least 2 hours, turning the pieces occasionally. Preheat broiler if manufacturer directs. Place chicken on rack in broiling pan; broil 35 minutes or until fork-tender, basting chicken pieces with marinade and turning occasionally with tongs. Serves 4.

## Chicken Portugal with Mushroom Sauce

-Portuguese-

| | |
|---|---|
| 1/2 pound mushrooms, thinly sliced | 1/4 cup all-purpose flour |
| 4 medium boneless chicken breasts | 1-1/2 cups whipping cream |
| 1 teaspoon salt | 1/3 cup white wine |
| 1/4 teaspoon pepper | 1/4 teaspoon ground nutmeg |
| | 1/2 cup butter or margarine |

In large skillet over medium-high heat, in hot margarine, cook mushrooms 5 minutes. With slotted spoon, remove into small bowl; set aside.

On waxed paper, combine flour, salt, pepper and nutmeg; dust chicken breasts with this mixture. In the same skillet with remaining butter, over medium-high heat, cook chicken breasts until golden on all sides.

Into the same skillet, stir in whipping cream, wine and mushrooms; heat to boiling. Reduce heat to low; cover and simmer 15 minutes or until chicken is fork-tender. Serves to: 4

## Pan-Fried Chicken with Creamy Gravy

| | |
|---|---|
| 1/4 cup all-purpose flour | 1/4 cup salad oil |
| 1 (3-pound) broiler fryer, cut up | Salt and pepper |

Cream Gravy:

| | |
|---|---|
| 1/4 cup all-purpose flour | 1 tablespoon dry or medium sherry |
| 2-1/2 cups milk | Salt and pepper to taste |
| 1 tablespoon chopped parsley | |

Dust chicken pieces on all sides with flour on waxed sheet. In medium skillet over medium heat, brown chicken pieces on all sides in hot oil, turning frequently. Sprinkle chicken lightly with salt and pepper. Reduce heat to medium-low heat. Cover; cook until fork-tender, about 25 minutes, removing cover for last few minutes to crisp skin. Remove them to warm platter.

Prepare gravy; pour off all but 1/4 cup drippings from skillet; blend in flour. Over medium heat, cook, stirring and scraping bits loose from skillet, until golden. Gradually stir in milk and cook, stirring constantly, until mixture is smooth and thickened. Stir in parsley and sherry, sprinkle salt and freshly ground pepper.

Serve chicken with some gravy poured over it, serve rest of the gravy in gravy boat. Serves 4.

## Circassian Chicken-Çerkez Tavugu

*-Circassian-*

*3 medium boneless chicken breasts*
*1/2 pound California walnuts*
*1-3/4 cups chicken broth*
*Olive oil for garnishing*

*1 teaspoon red pepper*
*3 dried bread slices, crumbled*
*Salt to taste*
*Red and black pepper to taste*

Çerkez Tavugu are moist chunks of cooked chicken bathed in a rich, smooth, beige-colored walnut sauce and garnished with red pepper, olive oil and whole walnuts. It is a popular party dish in Turkey.

In large saucepan over high heat, cover chicken with water; cook until chicken is tender. Reserve 1-3/4 cup fresh chicken broth to use later. Grind walnuts in food processor; add half of the red pepper and bread crumbs; grind it second time; add rest of the red pepper and bread crumbs, grind it one more time. Place walnut mixture into medium bowl.

Stir reserved chicken broth into walnut mixture gradually; sprinkle salt and red pepper to taste. Stir it gently, until walnut chicken broth mixture becomes like a thick gravy (walnut sauce). With sharp knife, cut chicken breasts into small bite-size pieces.

Sprinkle chicken pieces with salt and black pepper; pour walnut sauce over the chicken pieces. With teaspoon, sprinkle olive oil and red pepper over chicken. Garnish with whole walnut pieces. Serves 8.

## Baked Chicken

*10 medium garlic cloves*
*1-1/2 cups tarragon vinegar*
*1/4 cup sugar*
*2 tablespoons salad oil*
*2 tablespoons Worcestershire*

*4 teaspoons dry mustard*
*2 teaspoons salt*
*2 (3-pound) broiler-fryers,*
  *quartered*

Into large baking dish, crush garlic cloves and stir in next 6 ingredients. Add chicken pieces; turn pieces to coat them evenly in marinade. Cover; refrigerate at least 2 hours, turning chicken often. About 1-1/4 hours before serving, prepare outdoor grill for barbecuing. Place chicken on grill over medium coals; cook 35 minutes or until chicken is fork-tender, turning chicken frequently and basting occasionally with remaining marinade. Serves 8.

# Chicken Vienna

*-Austrian-*

1/2 cup butter or margarine
8 whole chicken breasts,
  skinned and boned
1/2 pound mushrooms,
  sliced

1/3 cup all-purpose flour
1/4 teaspoon salt
1 (13-3/4 ounce) can
  chicken broth
2 tablespoons half-and-half

In large skillet over medium-high heat, in 6 tablespoons hot butter or margarine, cook chicken, a few pieces at a time, until browned on all sides. Set chicken aside. In drippings over medium heat, in remaining 2 tablespoons butter, cook mushrooms until golden, about 5 minutes. With slotted spoon, remove mushrooms to small bowl. Into drippings, over medium heat, stir flour and salt until blended. Gradually stir in chicken broth and half-and-half and cook, stirring constantly, until mixture is thickened. Place chicken and mushrooms in sauce. Reduce heat to low; cover and simmer 25 minutes. Serves 8.


# Chicken Curry

*-Indian-*

2 tablespoons vegetable oil
3 whole boneless and skinless
  chicken breasts, split in half
2 medium-sized onions, chopped
2 tablespoons each of minced
  fresh ginger and garlic
3 tablespoons curry powder
1 tablespoon ground cumin
3 medium-sized tomatoes,
  chopped
2 cups chicken broth

1 pound red-skinned new potatoes
  cut in 1/4-inch dice
1 cup non-fat plain yogurt
1/2 cup chopped fresh mint
6 cups cooked rice pilaf (page 111)
1/2 cup each of golden raisins
  and toasted silvered almonds
8 fresh mint sprigs for garnish

In large heavy casserole in hot oil, over medium heat, sauté chicken about 4 minutes on each side, until pale golden. Remove and set aside. When cool enough to handle, cut into 1-inch cubes.

Add onions, ginger and garlic to casserole; sauté over low heat for 5 minutes. Sprinkle with curry powder and cumin; cook for 1 minute, stirring constantly.

Add tomatoes, chicken and broth. Bring to a simmer; reduce heat and cook, partially covered, for 30 minutes. Add potatoes; cook, uncovered, for 30 minutes. Ladle yogurt into small bowl and slowly whisk in 1 cup liquid from curry mixture; gradually stir back into curry. Heat through (do not boil). Stir in chopped mint. Serve over rice in bowls. Sprinkle raisins and almonds on top, if desired. Garnish with mint. Serves 6-8.

# Baked Chicken and Macaroni

2 (3-pound) whole chicken
1 (16-ounce) package macaroni
2 small onions, peeled
1/2 pound mushrooms, sliced
1/4 teaspoon black pepper
1/4 teaspoon ground nutmeg
Red pepper to taste
Salt
Water

1 tablespoon lemon juice
1/2 cup margarine
1/2 cup all-purpose flour
1/2 cup dry sherry (optional)
1 cup half-and-half
1-1/2 cups grated parmesan cheese

In large saucepan, cover chickens with water; add 1 onion, pepper and 1 tablespoon salt; over high-heat, heat to boiling. Reduce heat to low; cover and simmer 40 minutes or until fork-tender.

Place chickens on large plate. Strain chicken broth, reserve 3-1/2 cups (if you are not using sherry, reserve 4 cups). Cut chicken into large pieces; discard bones; cut into small chunks, set aside.

After cooking macaroni as package label directs; spread it out on a greased medium baking dish.

Chop remaining onion. In small saucepan over medium heat, with 2 tablespoons margarine, cook onion, mushrooms and lemon juice 5 minutes. Remove to medium bowl.

In the same saucepan, melt remaining margarine, when it is hot, stir flour, salt and red pepper to taste, nutmeg until mixture is smooth. Gradually stir this mixture in reserved chicken broth and cook stirring, until it is thickened.

Add half-and-half, chicken chunks and mushroom mixture and over low heat, cook, stirring, just until mixture is heated through. Spoon chicken mixture over macaroni in baking dish. Sprinkle on parmesan cheese and a pinch of red pepper.

Bake in 350 °F oven 30 minutes or until macaroni and chicken mixture are thoroughly heated and surface is golden. Serves 8-10.

## Chicken with Béchamel Sauce

*-French-*
*Béchamel sauce:*
*2 tablespoons all-purpose flour*
*2 tablespoons butter or margarine*
*1/2 teaspoon salt*
*1/8 teaspoon pepper*
*1/8 teaspoon red pepper*
*3 cups milk*

*4 chicken breasts,*
 *cut into bite-size pieces*
*2 large potatoes*
*3 carrots, sliced*
*2 tablespoons margarine*
*Salt to taste*
*Shredded Swiss cheese*
*Béchamel sauce*

Béchamel sauce: In medium saucepan over medium heat, melt butter or margarine; gradually add flour, stirring. Gradually, stir in milk; cook stirring until sauce is lightly thickened, add salt, pepper and continue to stir. Remove from heat.

In large saucepan over medium heat, in hot salad oil, cook potato cubes and sliced carrots; after they are slightly browned, add chicken pieces and salt to taste. Cook until vegetables and chicken fork-tender.

Generously grease large baking pan, spoon chicken-vegetable mixture into baking pan. Pour Béchamel sauce over chicken-vegetable mixture. Sprinkle with shredded Swiss cheese, bake in 350 °F oven until surface is golden. Serves 4.


## California-Style Herbed Lemon Chicken

*-American-*
*1 (3-pound) chicken, quartered*
*4 tomatoes*
*1/4 cup lemon juice*
*1/2 cup butter or margarine*
*2 teaspoons chopped parsley*

*1 teaspoon salt*
*1 teaspoon pepper*
*1 teaspoon sugar*
*1 teaspoon mixed spices*
 *(tableblend)*

In small saucepan over medium heat, heat butter, lemon juice, salt, sugar, mixed spices and pepper until butter is melted; set lemon mixture aside.

In large broiling pan, place chicken pieces, skin side down; broil 20 minutes. Baste with lemon mixture frequently to moisten and add flavor to chicken pieces.

Cut each tomato into 6 wedges. Turn chicken pieces, arrange tomatoes on the broiling pan.

Broil 15 to 20 minutes more. While broiling baste with lemon mixture frequently. Remove from broiler when chicken is tender. Garnish with parsley, serve with pan roasted potatoes. Serves 4.

# French Country Chicken

-French-
1 (5-pound) whole chicken
12 small new potatoes, peeled
3 medium carrots, trimmed
2 tablespoons unsalted butter
3 tablespoons salad oil
Salt and black pepper

20 tiny pearl onions
4 garlic cloves, crushed
1 bay leaf
Parsley stems
Sprigs of fresh thyme

Peel the potatoes and blanch for 5 minutes; drain and pat dry. Remove giblets and neck from inside of the bird; trim fat from the chicken. Rinse under running cold water; drain well.

Rub chicken with salad oil. In large open roasting pan, place chicken, breast side up. Roast, uncovered, in 325 °F oven 2-1/2 to 3 hours. When chicken turns golden cover loosely with a folded foil. Remove foil during last hour of roasting time. Brush bird generously with pan drippings and melted butter. Slice carrots. Add potatoes, sliced carrots, onions, garlic, thyme, bay leaf, salt and pepper. Cover and roast until chicken and vegetables are tender.

Remove chicken and place on serving platter. Baste with pan drippings and garnish with parsley leaves. Serves 6.

# Chicken Cordon Bleu

-French-
6 whole boneless chicken breasts
1 (8-ounce) package sliced,
  cooked ham or 2-1/2 cups
  sliced mushrooms
1 (8 oz.) package sliced Kraft
  deluxe Swiss cheese
3 tablespoons all-purpose flour
1 teaspoon paprika

Salt
2 tablespoons minced parsley
1/4 teaspoon garlic powder
1/2 cup white wine
1 chicken-flavor bouillon cube
1 tablespoon cornstarch
1 cup milk
6 tablespoons margarine

With meat mallet, pound each chicken breast until 1/4-inch thick. Lay out cheese and ham slices over the chicken breasts, add minced parsley, salt to taste and garlic powder; if you like, instead of adding ham slices, add sliced mushrooms; fold breasts over filling.

On flat surface, mix flour and paprika; coat chicken pieces with this mixture. Place in freezer open end down until firm, 5 to 10 minutes.

In large skillet over medium heat, in hot margarine, place chicken breasts open sides down; cook chicken until golden on all sides; cover and simmer until tender.

In small cup, stir cornstarch, 1/8 teaspoon salt and milk. In small saucepan over low heat, heat wine and bouillon; add cornstarch-milk mixture to heated wine and bouillon mixture, stir until mixture is thickened. Pour over filled chicken breasts and serve with vegetable-rice pilaf or baked potatoes. Serves 6.

# Chicken Milano

*-Italian-*

4 boneless chicken breasts, halved
1 pound shrimp, shelled and
  deveined
4 large tomatoes
1 (8-oz.) package mushroom, sliced
1 cup chopped onion
1 small garlic clove, minced

1/2 teaspoon salt
1 teaspoon basil
3 tablespoons chopped parsley
1/4 cup port wine
1/2 cup margarine

In large skillet over medium heat, in hot margarine, cook onion and garlic until tender. With slotted spoon, remove mixture to small bowl.

Rub chicken breasts with salt and pepper. In remaining margarine, cook chicken breasts until golden on all sides.

Peel and chop tomatoes, in small bowl, mash tomatoes until smooth. Pour mashed tomatoes, wine, basil, 3 tablespoons parsley and reserved onion mixture over chicken breasts; heat to boiling. Reduce heat to low; cover and simmer 10 minutes or until chicken is tender.

Add shelled shrimp and sliced mushroom; heat to boiling. Reduce heat to low; simmer a few minutes until shrimp are just pink and tender, stirring occasionally. Garnish with chopped parsley. Serves to: 6-8

# Chicken Kiev

4 whole boneless chicken breasts
1/2 cup butter
1 tablespoon chopped parsley
2 eggs
Salt
Pepper

2 garlic cloves, minced
1/2 teaspoon lemon juice
4 tablespoons all-purpose flour
2 tablespoons bread crumbs
Water
Salad oil

With meat mallet, pound chicken breasts to 1/4-inch thickness. In small bowl, mix butter, parsley, lemon juice, salt, pepper and minced garlic. Spread the garlic mixture over the chicken breasts. Fold them around the filling.

On waxed paper, mix flour and 1/2 teaspoon salt. In small bowl mix eggs and water. Place crumbs on another sheet of paper. Coat rolls with flour, egg, then crumbs. Place chicken rolls in freezer until firm, 5 to 10 minutes.

In 4-quart saucepan, heat 3-inches oil, place two breasts fry, 15 minutes or until browned and firm; drain. Repeat the process with the rest of the chicken breasts. Serve with winter salad. Serves 4.

# Chicken Croquettes

*-French-*
2-1/2 cups ground, cooked
  chicken
1 cup thick white cream sauce
2 tablespoons chopped
  parsley
1 tablespoon minced onion
1/2 teaspoon lemon juice
1/8 teaspoon rubbed sage

Salt
1 egg
1 tablespoon water
1/4 cup all-purpose flour
1/2 cup dried bread crumbs
Salad oil
Mushroom sauce or cheese sauce

*Cream Sauce:*
1/4 cup butter or margarine
1/4 cup all-purpose flour
1/2 teaspoon salt

1/8 teaspoon pepper
1/8 teaspoon paprika
1 cup milk or half-and-half

*Mushroom Sauce:*
1/4 cup butter or margarine
1/2 pound mushrooms, sliced
3/4 cup beef broth

3/4 teaspoon salt
1 tablespoon corn starch
1/4 cup sauterne

*Cheese Sauce:*
1 tablespoon butter or margarine
1 tablespoon all-purpose flour
1/4 teaspoon salt
Pepper to taste
Paprika to taste
1/2 cup milk or half-and-half

1/2 cup shredded cheddar cheese
1/8 teaspoon dry mustard

In medium bowl, blend well first six ingredients. Add salt to taste. Cover; chill several hours. About 30 minutes before serving: Shape chilled mixture into 8 patties. In shallow dish with fork, beat egg with water. Place flour and bread crumbs on separate sheets of waxed paper. Coat each croquette first in flour, then in crumbs. In 4-quart saucepan over medium heat, heat 1-inch oil to 370 °F. Fry croquettes until golden brown, turning frequently. Drain on paper towels; serve with the sauce you prefer.

Cream Sauce: In heavy medium saucepan over low heat, melt butter or margarine. Add flour, salt, pepper and paprika to melted butter or margarine. Over low heat, stir together until smooth. Gradually stir in milk; cook, stirring constantly, until thickened and smooth. Serve hot.

Mushroom Sauce: In medium skillet over medium heat, in hot butter or margarine, cook sliced mushrooms until tender, about 5 minutes, stirring occasionally. Stir in beef broth and salt; heat the mixture to boiling. Meanwhile, in cup, blend cornstarch and sauterne until smooth. Gradually stir sauterne mixture into mushroom mixture and cook, stirring constantly, until thickened. Serve mushroom sauce hot.

Cheese Sauce: Prepare cream sauce as above, into hot sauce, stir 1/2 cup shredded cheddar cheese and dry mustard. Cook over very low heat, stirring constantly, just until the cheese is melted. Serves 4.

## Chicken Pot Pie

2 (2-1/2 pound) broiler fryers,
  cut up
1/2 teaspoon pepper
1/2 teaspoon marjoram leaves
2 bay leaves
Water
Salt
2 large carrots, sliced
1 large celery stalk, sliced
3/4 pound small white onions

All-purpose flour
1-3/4 cups half-and-half
1 (10-ounce) package frozen
  baby lima beans, thawed
1/2 pound small mushrooms,
  each cut in half
Pastry for 2-piecrust (page 144)
1 egg yolk

In large Dutchoven, over high heat, heat first 4 ingredients, 4 cups water and 1 tablespoon salt to boiling. Reduce heat to low; cover and simmer 35 minutes or until chicken is fork tender. When chicken is done, reserve 1 cup broth. Cool chicken slightly; remove and discard bones and skin; cut meat into 1-inch pieces. In medium saucepan over high heat, heat carrots, celery, onions in reserved 1 cup broth to boiling. Reduce heat to low; cover and simmer 10 minutes. Remove from heat. Remove vegetables to small bowl, leaving broth in saucepan. In small bowl with fork, blend 1/3 cup flour with 3/4 cup half-and-half; gradually stir into broth in saucepan until smooth; stir in remaining half-and-half. Over low heat, cook, stirring constantly, until sauce is thickened. Stir in chicken, cooked vegetables, lima beans, mushrooms and 1-3/4 teaspoons salt. Spoon chicken mixture into medium baking dish. Preheat oven to 350 °F. Prepare pastry. On lightly floured surface with lightly floured rolling pin, roll dough into 14x10 rectangle. With knife, cut out small circle in center of pastry. Place pastry loosely over filling. With kitchen shears, trim edge, leaving 1-inch overhang; fold overhang under; make a high stand-up edge. In small bowl, mix well egg yolk with 1 teaspoon water. Brush pastry with egg-yolk mixture. Bake 1 hour or until crust is golden and mixture is hot. Serves 8.

# Chicken Monterey with Raisin-Almond Rice Pilaf

*Monterey Mushroom Stuffing:*
*1/3 cup water*
*1 chicken bouillon cube*
*1 teaspoon seasoned salt*
*1 teaspoon rubbed sage*
  *dash pepper*
*1 tablespoon butter or margarine*
*1-1/4 cups diced celery*
*3/4 cup diced carrots*
*2/3 cup chopped onion*

*6-ounces Portabella mushrooms*
  *chopped*
*6-ounces Portabellini mushrooms,*
  *chopped*
*5 slices slightly dry wheat bread, cubed*
*8 shiitake mushroom caps, sliced*

*Baked Chicken:*
*4 boneless chicken breasts*
*1/4 cup lemon juice*
*1/2 cup butter or margarine*

*1 teaspoon salt*
*1 teaspoon pepper*
*1 teaspoon sugar*

*Rice Pilaf with Raisins and Almonds:*
*4 cups raisin-almond rice pilaf (page 112)*
*Parsley leaves for garnish*

Monterey Mushroom Stuffing: Preheat oven to 350 degrees. In 3-quart saucepan heat together first 6 ingredients until bouillon cube is dissolved. Add celery, carrots and onion. Heat to boiling; reduce heat. Cover and simmer 5 minutes. Stir in mushrooms. Cover and simmer 5 minutes longer, stirring occasionally. Remove from heat. Add bread; mix until thoroughly moistened. Turn into shallow 1-1/2 quart baking dish. Bake 30 minutes or until top is dry.

Rice Pilaf with Raisins and Almonds: Prepare rice pilaf with raisins and almonds as on (page 112). In small skillet in hot butter, sauté sliced mushrooms; garnish rice pilaf with mushroom slices and parsley leaves.

Baked Chicken: Prepare chickens as on California style lemon herbed chicken. Do not use tomatoes (page 43).

Serve chickens with raisin-almond rice pilaf and Monterey mushroom stuffing. Serves 4.

## Stir-Fried Chicken with Cashews

*-Chinese-*
*2 large boneless chicken breasts*
*2 tablespoons salad oil*
*1 medium green pepper*
*1 small onion, sliced*
*1/2 teaspoon salt*
*1/4 teaspoon ground ginger*
*1 (16-ounce) can bean sprouts,*
  *drained*

*1/2 cup water*
*2 teaspoons corn starch*
*2 tablespoons soy sauce*
*3/4 cup cashews*
*1/2 tablespoons dry sherry*
*4 cups rice pilaf (page 111)*

Tenderize chickens with meat mallet; slice chickens crosswise into 1/2-inch wide strips; place them in small bowl; rub them with 1/2 tablespoon dry sherry; set aside.

Heat the wok; add salad oil; stir-fry (stirring quickly and frequently) green peppers, salt and ginger until green peppers are tender-crisp about 3 minutes. Remove cooked vegetables to hot plate.

With remaining oil; stir-fry chicken strips about 4 to 5 minutes. Add cooked vegetables, bean sprouts and water.

In small bowl, mix corn starch and soy sauce; pour into chicken-vegetable mixture in the wok; quickly stir-fry stirring frequently until mixture thickens.

Add toasted cashews and mix. Remove from the wok; serve over rice pilaf. Serves 4


## The Biltmore's Chicken Legs with Blue Cheese Sauce

*8 chicken legs*
*5 large Portabella mushrooms,*
  *sliced*
*1/4 cups lemon peels*
*2 tablespoons lemon juice*
*Butter or margarine*

*1/8 teaspoon garlic powder*
*Salt, black pepper and paprika to taste*
*Minced parsley, finely chopped chives*
*1-1/2 tablespoons lemon peel*
*1/2 cup crumbled blue cheese*
*1 cup milk*
*1 tablespoon all-purpose flour*

Remove half of the bones from legs, and excess skin; sprinkle with black pepper and salt (optional). In large grilling pan over medium-high heat, grill chicken pieces; 2 or 4 at a time, brush with melted butter while grilling, cover and keep them warm.

In small saucepan, over medium heat, in melted butter, blend 1 tablespoon all-purpose flour, stirring; add milk, blue cheese and garlic powder; cook stirring until well blended; add 1 teaspoon minced parsley; cook until slightly thickened.

In medium saucepan over medium-high heat, in hot butter, sauté sliced mushrooms, add lemon juice and stir. Before removing from heat, add lemon peel, mix gently; sprinkle with salt. Place 2 chicken legs on each plate, pour blue cheese sauce over them, garnish with chives and mushrooms. Serve with oven baked potatoes. Serves 4.

# Rock Cornish Hens with Mincemeat Dressing

2 (1-1/2 to 2 pounds) rock
   cornish hens, thawed
1/4 cup butter, melted
4 slices whole wheat bread
   cubed
3/4 cup orange juice
1/4 cup diced celery

1/2 cup prepared mincemeat,
   drained
1/2 teaspoon salt
2 tablespoons light corn syrup
2 teaspoons medium sherry

Remove giblets and necks from hens. Rinse hens under running cold water and drain. In open roasting pan, place hens breast side up. Roast, brushing occasionally with melted butter, in 325 °F oven about 1-1/4 hours or until a leg can be moved easily up and down.

For stuffing, in 1-quart casserole, combine bread cubes, orange juice, celery, mincemeat and salt; toss lightly. Bake along with hens for last 30 minutes roasting time.

In small bowl, mix corn syrup and sherry; during last ten minutes roasting time, brush over hens to glaze them. Serve stuffing with hens. Serves 4.


# Roast Duck à l'orange

*-French-*
1 (4-pound) duck
4 tablespoons sugar
1-1/2 tablespoons margarine
1 tablespoon corn starch
3 tablespoons orange extract
1-1/3 cups wine
Salt and pepper to taste

2 oranges, peeled
1 lemon
All-purpose flour
2 bay leaves
3 tablespoons vinegar
2-1/2 cups beef broth

Remove giblets and neck from duck. Rinse under running cold water and pat dry. Cut duck into quarters; sprinkle with pepper and salt. Place pieces, skin side down, on rack in 13x9-inch open roasting pan. Roast in 350 °F oven 1 hour; turn; roast 45 minutes more or until thickest part of drumstick feels soft when pinched with fingers.

In medium saucepan over medium heat, heat half of the margarine, bay leaves, salt and pepper; add wine. Meanwhile, peel oranges, add and heat to boiling. Discard bay leaves and orange peels. In another small saucepan heat orange and lemon juice and reduce to half. Heat remaining margarine; add flour; gradually add beef broth. Pour orange-lemon mixture into beef broth mixture and cook 10 minutes. Before removing saucepan, add orange extract and corn starch; stir well and cook until mixture thickens slightly. Place duck pieces on medium service plate. Serve with orange sauce. Serves 4.

## Quail Kabob

*-Turkish-*
*8 quails, rinsed*
*1 tablespoon butter*
*4 tomatoes, cut into wedges*

*4 bay leaves*
*Salt to taste*
*Pepper to taste*

Rinse quails under running cold water, pat dry. Sprinkle salt inside quails. Preheat broiler. Thread quails and tomato wedges with bay leaves alternately on metal skewers. Broil until quails are tender, brushing with melted butter occasionally. Serve with rice pilaf with vegetables. Serves 4.

## Turkey Roast with Waldorf Stuffing

*1 (2-pound) boneless fresh*
*  turkey breast roast*
*Glaze:*
*3 tablespoons sugar*
*4 teaspoons cornstarch*
*1-1/2 cups apple juice*
*3 tablespoons margarine*
*1/4 teaspoon ground allspice*

*Stuffing:*
*2 tablespoons margarine*
*1/4 cup thinly sliced celery*
*1/4 cup chopped onion*
*1/4 cup chopped apple*
*4 slices raisin bread, cut into*
*  1/2-inch cubes*
*1/4 teaspoon salt*
*1/4 teaspoon ground all spice*
*3 tablespoons apple juice*

Glaze: In small saucepan, combine sugar and cornstarch. Gradually, add 1-1/2 cups apple juice; cook and stir over medium-high heat until mixture bubbles and thickens. Remove from heat; stirring 3 tablespoons margarine and 1/4 teaspoon allspice; set aside.

Stuffing: In large skillet over medium-high heat, melt 2 tablespoons margarine. Add celery and onion; cook and stir 4 to 5 minutes or until crisp-tender. Add apple; cook an additional 1 minute. Stir in remaining stuffing ingredients, mixing gently. Set aside.

To make a pocket for stuffing, use long, sharp knife. Slash through the turkey breast roast lengthwise, cutting to within 1-inch of edges. Spoon stuffing into pocket.

Place turkey in 9x9-inch baking pan. Spoon 3/4 cup glaze over turkey; reserve remaining glaze. Cover loosely with foil. Roast at 350 °F 3 to 4 hours, basting occasionally with glaze mixture. Remove foil. Roast an additional 15 to 30 minutes. Let turkey stand 10 minutes before slicing. Heat and serve remaining glaze with turkey. Serves 8.

## Leman's Roast Turkey with Chestnuts

1 (12-pound) turkey, thawed
Salad oil
1/2 cup margarine
1/4 cup chopped fresh thyme
1/4 cup chopped parsley
1 tablespoon shredded onion
Water

15 to 20 chestnuts, cooked, peeled
1/2 cup water
Salt
Black pepper and paprika
1/2 teaspoon garlic powder
Rice pilaf with raisins and
  almonds (page 112)

In medium saucepan, boil chestnuts in water until soft inside. Rinse under running cold water, peel, place in small bowl; set aside.

Remove giblets and neck from inside turkey; rinse turkey under running cold water; drain well. In roasting pan, place turkey breast side up. Brush skin with salad oil.

Spicy mixture: In small saucepan over medium-high heat, cook onion and garlic for 5 minutes; add water, parsley, salt, pepper, paprika, chopped thyme; heat to boiling, about 5 minutes.

Pour spicy mixture over the turkey. In 325°F oven, roast 4 to 4-1/2 hours, covering with foil loosely when bird turns golden. Occasionally baste with spicy mixture. 1/2 hours before the bird is done, remove foil and baste turkey with pan drippings. If you use thermometer, turkey is done when it reads 180 °F.

Place bird on large serving plate, surround with raisin-almond rice pilaf and garnish with peeled chestnuts. Serves 8-12.

# VEGETABLES

## Mediterranean (Turkish) Style Vegetables Cooked with Olive Oil

In Turkey, there is a unique style of cooking which combines the pure flavors of vegetables and olive oil. These dishes are fairly easy to prepare. The vegetables are stewed in a mixture of olive oil, water and small amount of sugar. Sugar enriches the taste and preserves the texture of the vegetables. They are stewed in a pot with a tight-fitting lid until most of the water evaporates. This cooking process leaves behind a slightly sweet sauce uniquely flavored with olive oil and vegetables.

These vegetable dishes are served warm, lukewarm or cold, and always with fresh bread. They can be a full vegetarian meal or can be served alongside with a main course. They keep well in the refrigerator for several days.

## Vegetable Garnished Artichokes-Garnitürlü Enginar

*-Turkish-*
*12 to 15 large artichoke bottoms*
*1 medium potatoes, diced*
*1/2 cup sliced carrots*
*1/2 cup peas*
*3/4 cup chopped onion*
*7 cups water*

*1 lemon juiced*
*2 teaspoons sugar*
*Salt to taste*
*1/2 cup olive oil*
*2 tablespoons minced fresh dill*
   *to garnish*
*Lemon wedges*

Before start to cooking, see (page 55).This is a traditional Turkish dish; served as a first course or as a side dish. You can find canned large artichoke bottoms (Peeled, 2 to 3-inches in diameter) in some of supermarkets' international food sections and fresh large ones in farmer's markets. The largest fresh artichoke bottoms (Peeled, 3 to 4 inches diameter) can be found in The Mediterranean region, especially in Turkey. If you can not find artichoke bottoms you can use artichoke hearts.

Cut off stem and top; pull out all leaves; cut off hard parts of the skin; remove the fuzzy center part. Place large round shaped artichoke bottoms in small bowl filled with 7 cups water and lemon juice; set aside for 20 minutes.

In large saucepan over medium-high heat, in hot olive oil cook diced potatoes, thinly sliced carrots, peas and chopped onion for 2 to 3 minutes.

Add artichoke bottoms and lemon juice water, sugar and salt, over medium heat, cover and cook until artichokes are tender and water is absorbed.

Remove from heat; allow to cool completely; place on large serving plate. Spoon vegetables into the artichoke bottoms. From saucepan, spoon lemon and vegetable flavored juice over the artichokes. Garnish with minced fresh dill and serve with lemon wedges. Serves 6-8.

## Green Beans Cooked with Olive Oil-Zeytinyagli Taze Fasulye

*-Turkish-*

| | |
|---|---|
| 1-1/2 pounds green beans | 1/4 teaspoon salt |
| 1 large onion, chopped | 1/2 teaspoon pepper |
| 2 large tomatoes, diced | 1 teaspoon sugar |
| 3/4 olive oil or salad oil | Water |

Before cooking, see (page 55). Rinse green beans under running cold water, drain; trim ends and cut into 2-inch length pieces. If you desire cut these lengthwise also.

In large Dutchoven over medium heat, in sizzling olive oil, sauté chopped onions until tender. Add diced tomatoes; cook until soft, about 2 to 3 minutes. Add green beans, oil, salt, sugar, pepper and water to cover the beans. Cover and over medium heat, cook until beans are tender and most of the water is absorbed. Remove from heat. Ladle beans into medium serving bowl and cool completely. Garnish with chopped parsley. Serve cold and with the main course. Serves 8.

## Imam's Delight-Imam Bayildi

*-Turkish-*

| | |
|---|---|
| 6 long and slim-Mediterranean or 12 Japanese eggplants | 1-1/3 cups olive oil or salad oil |
| 2 to 3 small onions | 3 large tomatoes |
| 4 cups water | 6 garlic cloves, minced |
| 1/4 cup minced parsley | 1 tablespoon sugar |
| Salt to taste | Water |

Before cooking this dish, see (page 55). This is a traditional Turkish dish, served as a first course.

Peel lengthwise strips of skin from eggplants, to give striped effect. Place eggplants in large bowl, cover with salted water; set aside for 20 minutes.

Meanwhile peel tomatoes and cut into small cubes. Chop or slice onions. In large bowl, mix tomatoes, sliced onion, minced garlic, minced parsley, and salt.

Drain eggplants, if you are using Japanese eggplants, cut, open eggplant's lengthwise from 1/2-inch of the top and bottom. If you are using long and slim Mediterranean eggplants cut them in half and repeat the same process to open. Remove any large seeds from eggplant. Gently open and fill in each eggplant with tomato mixture.

Place stuffed eggplants in large saucepan; add water, olive oil, sugar and salt. Over medium heat, cook until eggplants are tender and water is absorbed. Garnish with parsley, serve cold before the main course. Serves 4-6.

## Asparagus Mornay

1-1/2 pound asparagus  
1 small garlic clove  
3 tablespoons all-purpose flour  
2 tablespoons chopped chives  
2-1/2 cups milk  

1/2 stick butter, melted  
Salt  
3/4 cup grated cheddar cheese  
A pinch of ground nutmeg  

Hold base of stalk firmly and bend stalk; break off end where it is too tough to eat; discard end. With sharp knife, trim scales if stalks are gritty.

In large saucepan over medium heat, in boiling salted water, heat stalks to boiling; reduce heat to low; cover and simmer until tender-crisp, about 5 minutes.

Sauce Mornay: In small saucepan, over medium heat, in melted butter add flour; cook 1 to 2 minutes, stirring. Sprinkle milk with salt and add gradually to the saucepan; stir frequently, bring to boil. Remove from heat and stir in grated cheddar cheese, chives and ground nutmeg; stir well.

Arrange asparagus on large heat-proof serving dish. Pour sauce over and sprinkle with remaining cheddar cheese and grill until golden. Serve individually as a first course. Serves 4-6.

## Zucchini Fritters-Kabak Mücveri

-Turkish-  
3 large zucchinis  
2 eggs  
1/4 teaspoon salt  
2 teaspoons dried dill  
1 teaspoon minced parsley  

1/8 teaspoon pepper  
1/2 cup shredded Swiss cheese  
1/2 cup all-purpose flour  
1/4 teaspoon onion powder  
  (optional)  
Salad oil  

Usually served as a side dish. Grate zucchini; place in colander; sprinkle with salt and let drain 15 minutes.

Squeeze out moisture and pat with paper towels; place zucchini in large bowl and add eggs, onion, dill, parsley, cheese, flour, pepper and salt; mix well.

In large skillet, over medium-high heat, in 1/4-inch deep hot salad oil, drop the batter by rounded tablespoonfuls into pan, allowing space between fritters. Fry for 2 minutes on one side then brown the other side; with slotted spatula transfer the fritters to paper towel to drain. Repeat same process with remaining batter. Arrange fritters on serving plate. Serve with the main course. Serves 4.

# Stuffed Grape Leaves-Zeytinyagli Yaprak Dolma

*-Turkish-*

| | |
|---|---|
| *4-1/2 cups rice* | *1 tablespoon allspice* |
| *1 medium onion* | *2 tablespoons cinnamon* |
| *1/2 cup pine nuts* | *2-1/2 tablespoons sugar* |
| *1 cup currants* | *Salt to taste* |
| *1 to1-1/3 cups olive oil* | *1/2 lemon, juiced* |
| *3 tablespoons dried dill* | *1 pound grape leaves* |
| *3 tablespoons minced parsley* | *9-1/2 to 10 cups water* |
| *2 tablespoons dried mint* | |

This is a traditional Turkish dish that is served as a side dish along with the main course. It is also a popular party dish. In Turkish, "Stuffed grape leaves cooked with olive oil" is called "Zeytinyagli Yaprak Dolma". The word "Stuffed" means in Turkish "Dolma, doldurulmus". Because this dish is cooked without meat, sometimes it is called "Fake Dolmas-Yalanci Dolma". The word "Fake" means in Turkish "Yalanci". "Dolmas" or stuffed grape leaves, come with two types of filling: Rice or meat and rice (page 70). The same rice mixture can be used to stuff mussels, vegetables such as peppers, eggplants, cooked cabbage leaves, tomatoes and zucchini.

In large saucepan, over low heat cook onions and until they are translucent about 10 to 15 minutes. Do not add water or oil while cooking onion.

Add half of the olive oil and pine nuts, over medium heat, cook until pine nuts slightly golden. Add rice, dried mint, raisins, salt and sugar; stir to mix.

Add 5 cups water, cover, over medium-low heat, simmer until liquid is absorbed. Remove from the heat and add cinnamon, allspice, dried dill, and parsley. Stir well.

Remove grape leaves from jar and immerse in boiling water about 30 seconds; drain and rinse under running cold water. Cut off and discard tough stems; pat leaves to dry. Place shiny side down on a flat surface. Place a rounded teaspoon of the rice mixture on the center of the leaf. Fold base end of leaf over filling to cover; fold in both sides of leaf, overlapping them, then roll up carefully to form a sealed cylinder about 2 to 3-inches long. Repeat the same process with remaining leaves and filling. Cover bottom of a 12-inch Dutchoven or heavy, broad bottomed pan with a layer of remaining leaves; arrange a layer of stuffed leaves, seam side down close together. Sprinkle with some of the lemon juice and some of remaining olive oil. Repeat, making layers to accommodate all of the stuffed leaves. Suggested number of layers is 2 to 3. Sprinkle each layer with remaining lemon juice and olive oil, being careful not to disturb layers. Add remaining 4-1/2 to 5 cups of water.

Place heavy plate on top to weight down stuffed leaves. Cover and simmer over low heat until rice is tender, about 40 minutes. To test, open one of the pockets. Remove from the heat and lift stuffed leaves out with slotted spoon. Arrange on platter and cool completely. Serve with lemon wedges. Makes 100 dolmas.

## Pinto Beans Cooked with Olive Oil-Zeytinyagli Barbunya

-Turkish-

1 pound pinto beans
1 medium green pepper (optional) thinly sliced
2 small onions, chopped
3 medium tomatoes, peeled and diced

3/4 cup olive oil
2 teaspoons sugar
Salt to taste
2 tablespoons minced parsley
4 cups water
Water

Before start to cooking see (page 55). This is a Turkish dish served as a first course or a side dish. In large Dutchoven, over high heat, boil beans, water and salt for 2 minutes. Set aside for 1 hour. Drain; and place in large bowl.

Meanwhile, in Dutchoven over medium heat, in hot oil, cook peppers for 2 minutes; stirring frequently. Remove peppers with slotted spoon into small bowl.

In remaining oil cook chopped onions, until tender; add tomatoes. Then add drained beans, peppers, salt, sugar and 4 cups water. Over medium heat, cover and cook until beans are tender and water is absorbed. While cooking, if it is necessary add hot water. Remove from heat; ladle into large serving bowl and cool completely; Garnish with chopped parsley and serve with lemon wedges. Serves 8-10.


## Spinach Casserole

2-1/2 tablespoons margarine
3 tablespoons all-purpose flour
1 (9-oz.) package frozen chopped spinach, thawed and drained
1/2 cup shredded Swiss cheese
1 small onion, chopped

1/4 teaspoon salt
1/2 teaspoon pepper
6 tablespoons corn bread crumbs
1-1/2 cups milk
2 medium eggs

In large saucepan, over medium heat, cook 2 tablespoons margarine and flour about 5 minutes. Gradually add milk and stir to mix. Remove from heat; cool; add 2 eggs and mix well.Sprinkle with salt and pepper. Cook, over medium heat until mixture thickens.

In small saucepan, over medium heat, in 1/2 tablespoon hot margarine, sauté onions until tender. Add drained spinach and cook about 15 minutes. Set aside.

Grease large baking pan; pour half of the milk mixture into pan. Spread spinach in the middle; sprinkle bread crumbs over the spinach and pour in remaining milk mixture. Sprinkle shredded Swiss cheese over the casserole. In 400 °F oven, bake until top is golden, about 30 to 40 minutes. Serve with the main chicken or meat dishes. Serves 4-6.

# Okra Stew-Bamya

*-Turkish-*
*2 pounds okra*
*1 small onion, chopped*
*1 large tomatoes, peeled and*
  *diced*
*2 tablespoons margarine*

*1/4 teaspoon salt*
*1/8 teaspoon pepper*
*Water*

Rinse and cut the okra heads in apple peeling fashion. Do not cut deep in order to avoid releasing the sticky juice.

In large saucepot over medium heat, in hot margarine sauté chopped onions. Add peeled and diced tomato; cook until tomatoes are tender. Add okra, salt, pepper and water to cover.

Cover and cook until okra are tender, about 20 to 30 minutes. Serve with lemon wedges. Serves 4.

# MEAT

## Leman's Filet Mignon with Mustard Caper Sauce

-French-

3 tablespoons butter
6 filet mignon steaks
1/2 cup dry vermouth
2 tablespoons chopped
  green onions
1/2 cup water
1/2 heavy whipping cream

2 tablespoons capers
2-1/2 teaspoons mustard
3/4 teaspoon salt
1/2 teaspoon coarsely
  ground black pepper
1 beef-flavor bouillon cube

In large skillet over medium-high heat, in hot butter, cook steaks until both sides are browned. Reduce heat and cook until desired doneness. Remove steaks to warm plate.

Reduce heat to medium; add vermouth and green onions to remaining drippings. Cook about 2 minutes. Stir in water, heavy cream, capers, mustard, salt, ground pepper and bouillon cube. Heat sauce to boiling.

Serve the sauce separately. If you like serve with roasted potatoes and vegetables. Serves 6.

## Herbed Ground Beef Stuffed Eggplants-Karniyarik

-Turkish-

6 slim medium size eggplants
1/2 pound ground beef
3 medium tomatoes, peeled,
  diced
1 onion, peeled, chopped
3 tablespoons minced parsley

1/2 teaspoon mixed spices(tableblend)
1-1/2 tablespoons margarine
2 cups water
Salt and pepper to taste
Olive oil

This is a traditional Turkish dish in which slim and tender eggplants are stuffed with seasoned ground beef and garnished with sliced tomatoes and peppers. You can find slim medium size eggplants from local farmers markets or in Middle Eastern grocery stores. If you cannot find slim eggplants, you can use 12 Japanese eggplants.

Remove stems; peel lengthwise strips of skin from eggplants, to give striped effect. Place in salted water for 15 minutes. Pat dry eggplants; cut to open lengthwise from 1/2-inch top and bottom of edges. Remove any excess of seeds from the center. In large skillet, in hot oil, cook until they are soft and golden. Remove cooked eggplants and set aside. Meanwhile, in medium skillet, in 1 tablespoon margarine, sauté chopped onions until they are translucent. Add ground beef and cook for 4 minutes. Add salt, pepper, mixed spices, diced tomatoes and minced parsley. Cook until most of the liquid is absorbed. Remove from heat. Place eggplants in large skillet. Fill each eggplant with ground beef mixture. Add water, margarine and salt to taste. Top each stuffed eggplant with peeled and sliced tomatoes. Cover and cook until most of the liquid is absorbed. Serves 6.

## Steak au Poivre

-French-

4 beef tenderloins
3 teaspoons mixed peppercorns, crushed
3 tablespoons butter

2 tablespoons salad oil
4 tablespoons cognac or brandy
1/2 cup double cream
1/4 teaspoon salt

Place steaks on flat surface. Sprinkle with the crushed peppercorn and press into both sides of meat. In large frying pan, heat the butter and cooking oil.

Add meat and cook the both sides; reduce the heat, cook to personal liking. Remove the steaks from pan and place on warm plate.

Meanwhile, add the brandy to the frying pan and flambe. As soon as flames have died down, add cream and salt. Gradually bring to a boil while stirring. Simmer for 4-5 minutes, pour over steaks and serve. Serve with roasted potatoes or potato casserole. Serves 4.

## Barbecued Beef Tenderloin with Marmaris Style Baked Potato

-Turkish-

4 medium beef tenderloins
2 tablespoons minced parsley
1/2 cup melted butter
Salt
Pepper
Mixed spices

4 large potatoes
1-1/2 cups shredded gruyère
1 large garlic clove, minced
4 green onions, minced
1 cup sour cream

Marmaris is a beautiful holiday town on the southwest coast of Turkey.

In small bowl, mix sour cream, minced garlic clove, 1/2 teaspoon salt, 1 teaspoon mixed spices, minced onions and 4 tablespoons of melted butter. Mix well and set aside.

Preheat oven to 375°F. Wash potatoes and pat dry, place in shallow pan. Bake 60 minutes or until fork-tender.

Meanwhile, prepare barbecue grill for cooking. In small cup, mix the rest of the melted butter, 1/2 teaspoon salt and 1/4 teaspoon pepper. Brush steaks with this mixture and barbecue them until the steaks are of desired doneness.

Remove potatoes from the oven; wrap them with aluminum foil and slash the tops; pressing from both sides to open wider. With fork mash the potatoes, add herbed sour cream mixture, and mix until well blended with potato. Spoon shredded gruyère equally on each wrapped potato. Place potatoes in 350 °F oven for 5 to 7 minutes or until the cheese is melted. Garnish with green onions and parsley. Serve with the steaks. Serves 4.

# Châteaubriand with Béarnaise Sauce

*-French-*

2 (2-pound) Châteaubriand
  tenderloin roasts
8 large artichokes
2 teaspoons salt
4 medium carrots
1 pound medium mushrooms
2 (14 oz.)cans hearts of palm,
  drained
1 tablespoon butter
Lemon slices

*Béarnaise Sauce:*
4 tablespoons red wine vinegar
2 tablespoons chopped parsley
3 teaspoons chopped
  green onion
3 teaspoons tarragon
1/4 teaspoon cracked black
  pepper corns
6 small egg yolks
1-1/4 cups butter, softened

Preheat the broiler, sprinkle roast with salt. Place both pieces of meat on rack in broiling pan; broil 30 minutes for rare or until the desired doneness, turning once.

Prepare artichokes: cut off stem and top, trim thorny tips of leaves and pull loose leaves from around bottom of artichoke. In large saucepot over medium heat, in boiling, salted water, place artichokes on their stem ends. Add a few lemon slices, heat to boiling, cover saucepot, reduce heat to low and cook about 30 minutes or until leaf can be pulled out easily. With spoon, scoop out choke from cooked artichokes. Fill the centers with Béarnaise sauce.

Béarnaise Sauce: In double-boiler top, combine first 4 ingredients. Over high heat, heat to boiling. Boil until vinegar is reduced to about 2 tablespoons. Place double-boiler top over double-boiler bottom containing hot, not boiling, water. Add egg yolks and cook, beating constantly with wire whisk until slightly thickened. Add butter, about 2 tablespoons at a time, beating constantly with whisk, until butter is melted and mixture is thickened. Stir in parsley. Serve about 1 tablespoon hot sauce over broiled Châteaubriand. Makes 2 cups Béarnaise sauce. Béarnaise sauce can be served with tenderloin, filet mignon, flank steak and poached or baked fish.

Garnishing: In small saucepan over high heat, boil sliced carrots until tender. Place carrots in small plate. Discard remaining water. In small saucepan, over medium heat, in hot butter sauté whole mushrooms until just tender.

If you like, slice meat; arrange meat on serving platter and surround with sliced carrots, hearts of palms and sautéed mushrooms. Ladle warm Béarnaise sauce into prepared artichoke bowls, serve alongside meat. Serves 8.

## Flank Steak Stuffed with Mushrooms

1-pound beef flank steak
1/2 pound mushrooms, sliced
2 small onions, sliced
1 tablespoon minced parsley

1/2 teaspoon pepper
1/4 cup red wine
1 tablespoon all-purpose flour
Water

With large sharp knife, score the steak to make a diamond pattern on both sides; sprinkle the steak with pepper. In small bowl, combine wine, mushrooms, onions, parsley and flour. Mix well. Spread evenly on one side of steak, leaving 1-inch border. Roll steak from long side and secure with wooden picks. On waxed paper, dust meat lightly with flour. Place the steak on greased baking pan; add 2 tablespoons melted butter and 1 cup water to pan cover with foil and bake in 375 °F oven 40 minutes or until the steak is tender. Remove cover and bake 20 minutes or until the top is browned. Serve with rice pilaf with tomatoes. Serves 4.

## Beef Stew with Vegetables

2-1/2 pound beef for stew
1/4 cup all-purpose flour
3 tablespoons margarine
1 large onion, chopped
1 garlic clove, minced
3 cups water
4 beef bouillon cubes
3/4 teaspoon salt
Parsley, minced

1 tablespoon cooking wine
1/4 teaspoon pepper
4 medium potatoes,
  cut in chunks
1 (16-ounce) bag carrots, sliced
1/2 pound okra (optional)
1 (10-0unce) package frozen peas
3 medium zucchini, sliced
2 medium tomatoes, cut into chunks

Cut meat into 1-inch chunks. In large Dutchoven, over medium-high heat, in 2 table spoons hot margarine, brown the meat chunks; 1/3 of the meat chunks at a time. Remove pieces as they brown.

Reduce heat to medium. Into remaining meat juices, add onion and garlic; cook for 2 minutes; stir in flour. Gradually add water, salt, wine and pepper; cook, stirring until mixture is slightly thickened.

Add meat; heat to boiling, stirring. Reduce heat to low; cover; simmer 2 hours until almost tender, stirring occasionally.

Peel the head of the okra, do not peel deeply enough to open the sticky juice passages. Add potatoes and carrots; over medium heat, heat to boiling. Reduce heat to low; cover and simmer 10 minutes; add zucchini, okra and tomatoes.

10 minutes later, add peas; cover and simmer 5 to 10 minutes longer or until all the vegetables are tender. Serves 8-10.

## Flambéed Pepper Steak

-French-
4 beef tenderloin or sirloin steaks
4 teaspoons green peppercorns
1 small onion
1 tablespoon butter or margarine
1 teaspoon salt

2/3 cup whipping cream
3 tablespoons beef consomme
3 tablespoons cognac or brandy

Crush green peppercorns in mortar with pestle. Chop onion and combine with peppercorns. Press pepper corn mixture into meat on both sides. In large skillet, heat butter until lightly brown. Add steaks. Brown well on one side, turn steaks over, and brown on other side. Sprinkle lightly with salt. Remove steaks to serving dish; cover and keep warm.

Add cream to skillet, scrape up brownings, cook until reduced. Add beef consomme, strain liquid; set aside. Rinse skillet and heat skillet again. Add steaks; pour cognac over. Ignite; add cream mixture. Let cook for 1 to 2 minutes. Serve with vegetables, Pommes Anna and red wine. Serves 4.

## Beef Stew Provençal Style

-French-
3 pounds lean boneless beef
  cut in 2-inch cubes
16 small onions, 1-inch
  diameter
5 medium carrots, cut in
  3/4-inch pieces
1/2 teaspoon dried thyme
  rosemary and summer
  savory

2 bay leaves
2-1/2 cups dry red wine
1 cup frozen peas, thawed
2-1/2 tablespoons cornstarch
  and water, combined
Salt and pepper to taste
2 tablespoons margarine

This is a traditional dish from Provence area, France. In large kettle, in 2 tablespoons margarine, cook beef and brown on all sides. Stir in onions, carrots, thyme, rosemary, savory, bay leaves and wine. Bring to a boil, cover and simmer until meat is very tender, 2-1/2 to 3 hours. Lift out meat and vegetables. Discard fat from pan juices; measure 2 cups juices. Add peas to juices and bring to a boil. Add cornstarch and water, and cook, stirring, until sauce thickens. If necessary add more water. Season to taste, with salt and pepper. Pass sauce with meat and vegetables. Serves 10.

# Tenderloin with Whiskey Peppercorn Sauce

*-French-*

| | |
|---|---|
| 4 tenderloin steaks | 1/4 cup whiskey |
| 5 tablespoons butter | 2 cups milk |
| 1 tablespoon mixed peppercorn | 2 tablespoons all purpose flour |
| Salt to taste | 1/2 teaspoon tarragon |

Crush 1/2 tablespoon mixed peppercorns in mortar with pestle. Sprinkle meat with crushed peppercorns. In large skillet, heat butter until lightly brown. Add steaks. Brown well on one side, turn steaks over, brown other side. Add 6 tablespoons water cover and simmer until desired doneness. Sprinkle with salt, remove steaks to warm platter and cover. Reserve remaining liquid. In small saucepan, in 1 tablespoon hot butter, add 2 tablespoons flour, cook, stirring. Gradually add 2 cups milk and reserved liquid, 1/4 cup whiskey and 1/2 teaspoon tarragon, salt and 1/2 tablespoon mixed peppercorn; cook, stirring until mixture is slightly thickened. Serve steaks with sauce, vegetables, roast potatoes and pasta radiatore. Serves 4.

# Ladies Thigh-Kadinbudu Köfte

*-Turkish-*

| | |
|---|---|
| 1/2 pound lean ground beef | 1 bunch fresh parsley |
| 3 medium onions, minced | 1 bunch fresh dill |
| 3 tablespoons olive oil | 1/8 teaspoon oregano |
| 3/4 cup cooked rice (page 111) | Salad oil for cooking |
| 1/2 cup shredded Swiss cheese | 3/4 cup all-purpose flour |
| 2 medium eggs | Bread crumbs |

Kadinbudu köfte is one of the interesting forms of ground meat cookery. The Middle East is the only part of the world where the meatball is truly exalted.

In large skillet over medium heat, in hot olive oil cook onions until tender. Add half of the ground beef. With a back of spoon mix thoroughly, cooking until all juice is absorbed. Remove from heat.

In large bowl, combine cooked ground beef mixture, and the rest of the ground beef; mix it well. Add cooked rice, 1 egg, shredded Swiss cheese, minced dill and parsley, oregano, pepper and salt.

Place in large saucepan, over medium heat, cook for 5 to 7 minutes. Remove batter into large bowl. Place 2 tablespoons ground beef mixture in your palm and make a ball shape and then press it between your hands to make an oval shape. On waxed paper, dust the oval shaped ground beef mixtures (köftes) with flour, then coat with mixed egg and then coat with bread crumbs. In large skillet over medium heat, in hot salad oil, cook until both sides until golden crisp. Serve lukewarm or cold with lemon wedges. Serves 4-6.

## Herbed Ground Beef Kabob-Köfte

*-Turkish-*
1 pound ground beef
2 tablespoons bread crumbs
2 tablespoons minced parsley
1/2 small onion, minced
1 teaspoon cumin

1/4 teaspoon salt
1/8 teaspoon pepper
1/8 teaspoon red pepper
2 to 3 tablespoons salad oil or
    margarine for frying
1/2 teaspoon olive oil (optional)

Turkish cuisine features innumerable varieties of köfte; this is one them; you may barbecue or fry in pan.

In large bowl, combine ground beef, bread crumbs, parsley, onion, salt, black and red pepper and olive oil; mix thoroughly by hand.

Place 1-1/2 tablespoonful meat mixture in your palm, squeeze, first making a ball shape; then flattening. Repeat the same process with the rest of the ground beef mixture. In large frying pan over medium-high heat, in hot oil or margarine, cook until one side is browned. Turn and cook the other sides. If you like, serve with French fries or oven-baked potatoes and eggplant salad. Serves 4.

## Deluxe Beef Pockets

*-French-*
1 pound mushrooms, minced
1/4 cup butter or margarine
1 medium onion, minced
3 cups fresh bread crumbs
1/2 teaspoon pepper
Water

1/4 teaspoon thyme leaves
1 teaspoon salt
Pastry for 4 (2-crust pies) (page 144)
1 (4-pound) beef rib eye roast
2 eggs, separated

In large frying pan, over medium heat, in hot butter, cook minced mushrooms and onion 5 minutes or until all liquid is evaporated. Stir in bread crumbs, pepper, thyme and salt; cool.

Prepare pastry and divide into 5 equal pieces. Trim all the fat; Cut meat in half lengthwise; slice each half crosswise into 5 equal pieces. In large skillet, over medium heat, cook 5 minutes each side. Remove from heat; sprinkle with salt. On floured surface, roll 1 piece pastry to 14x11, cut 2 rectangles 6-1/2x10; reserve scraps. Place 1/3 cup of mushroom mixture in center of pastry rectangle and place a piece of meat on top. In bowl with fork, beat egg whites with 2 tablespoons water. Brush pastry edges with mixture. Fold pastry over meat and mushroom mixture; overlapping edges. Press to seal and place on cookie sheet. Refrigerate while preparing the rest of the pockets.

Roll out pastry scraps and with sharp knife, cut into leaf shapes. Brush backs with egg white and arrange on the top of the pockets. Preheat the oven to 400 °F. In cup, beat egg yolks with 2 teaspoons water and brush over pastry. Bake 30 minutes. Serves 10.

## Stuffed Vegetables-Etli Dolma

*-Turkish-*

| | |
|---|---|
| 3 large zucchini | 1/4 teaspoon salt |
| 3 small green bell peppers | 1/2 teaspoon pepper |
| 3 medium tomatoes | 1 teaspoon mixed spices |
| 3 tablespoons margarine | 1/4 cup rice |
| 1 small onion, minced | 1 tablespoon minced fresh dill |
| 1 pound ground beef | 2 tablespoons all-purpose flour |

Turkish bell peppers and zucchini have a different texture and taste than those grow in America. Turkish bell peppers are thinner, have a richer taste and have lighter green color than those grown in America.

Rinse the zucchini, cut off ends and cut each zucchini width-wise into half (you will have 6 halves of zucchini to fill), remove and discard seeds, reserving the center parts. Cut off tops of the peppers, discard seeds and reserve tops to cover. Rinse tomatoes, cut off tops and reserve to cover. Remove seeds and juice and reserve juice.

Blend reserved zucchini pieces, tomato pieces and its juice and flour. Place in small cup and set aside. In small saucepan over medium heat, sauté onions, in hot margarine until onion is tender. Add rice and 2 to 3 tablespoons water and cook until water is absorbed about 5 to 7 minutes.

Remove from heat and cool. Place in large plate, add ground beef, parsley, salt, pepper, mixed spices and mix thoroughly by hand. Stuff peppers, tomatoes and zucchini with the ground beef-rice mixture; cover the tops with the reserved tomato and pepper tops parts.

In large Dutchoven, heat margarine, add flour and vegetable-juice mixture and; put in the stuffed vegetables, adding water just to cover. Over medium heat, cook until vegetables are tender. Sprinkle with dill. Serve hot with plain yogurt. Serves 4.

## Deluxe Guacamole Hamburger

| | |
|---|---|
| 1/2 to 3/4 pound ground beef | 1 medium avocado |
| 2 tablespoons minced parsley | 1 large tomatoes |
| 1/4 teaspoon cumin | 1/2 large onion, sliced |
| 1 small onion, shredded | into large rings |
| Salt, cayenne and black | 4-6 lettuce leaves |
| pepper to taste | Grey Poupon mustard |
| 1 small garlic clove, minced | French fries for 4 |

Mix ground beef, parsley, cumin, shredded onion, salt and cayenne and black pepper to taste. Make 4 large burgers. Meanwhile, prepare barbecue. Grill burgers to the desired doneness. In small bowl mash, peeled avocados; add mustard and minced garlic. Mix well. Set aside. Prepare hamburger buns and spread with the avocado mixture (California version of guacamole), top with tomato and onion rings and lettuce leaves. Serve hamburgers with beer and French fries. Serves 4.

# Meat Loaf

2 pound lean ground beef
2 small onions, minced
Salt to taste
Pepper to taste
2-1/2 tablespoons margarine
1 tablespoon tomato paste

1 cups fresh bread crumbs
2 eggs
3 hard cooked eggs
1/4 cup peas
1 medium carrot, peeled, sliced
Water

In large bowl, mix ground beef, bread crumbs, minced onion, 2 eggs, pepper and salt to taste. Spread this mixture on waxed paper; give a 1-inch thick rectangular shape. In small saucepan over medium-high heat, in water cook carrot slices and peas until tender.

Place lengthwise cooked eggs, cooked carrot slices and peas on one side. Fold the beef over the fillings; close the open ends. Grease large baking pan; place meat loaf in baking pan seam side down. Bake in 350 °F oven until loaf is done or about 40 minutes. Remove pan from the oven; spoon pan drippings in small cup; add tomato paste and 3/4 cup water and mix well. Slice meat loaf and pour the tomato mix over it and bake for 5 minutes. Serves 8.


# Meatball Minestrone

-Italian-
1 (10-ounce) package frozen
  chopped spinach, thawed
1-1/2 pound lean ground beef
1/3 cup fine dry bread crumbs
1 egg
1/4 teaspoon pepper
1 tablespoon vegetable oil
1 large onion, finely chopped
1 garlic clove, minced or pressed

1/2 teaspoon dry oregano and basil
7 cups unsalted chicken broth
1 (14-1/2 ounce) unsalted stewed
  tomatoes undrained
1 (15-1/4 ounce) kidney beans, undrained
1 cup thinly sliced carrots and celery
1 cup rotelle or other pasta twists
Salt to taste

Squeeze moisture from spinach. Combine spinach, beef, crumbs, egg and pepper. Form 1-inch balls. Place meatballs well apart on rimmed nonstick baking pan. Bake in 500 °F oven until browned, 6 to 8 minutes.

In large Dutchoven over medium heat, in hot oil, sauté onion, garlic until tender about 5 to 6 minutes; add 1/4 teaspoon oregano and 1/4 teaspoon basil. Cook stirring until limp. Add broth, chopped tomatoes and beans; cover and simmer 10 minutes. Add carrots and celery; boil gently 10 minutes.

Add pasta; cover and cook just until tender. Add meat balls and heat through. Sprinkle with salt. Serves 6.

## Beef Bourguignonne

-French-

3 pounds beef for stew,
  cut into 2-inch chunks
15 pearl onions
All-purpose flour
1 large carrot, chopped
1 large onion, chopped
1/4 cup brandy
1 pound mushrooms, sliced

2 garlic cloves, crushed
1-1/2 teaspoons salt
1/2 teaspoon thyme
1/4 teaspoon pepper
1 bay leaf
3 cups burgundy
Butter or margarine

In large Dutchoven, over medium-high heat, cook small white onions until lightly browned. Remove onions to small bowl, set aside.

In drippings, in Dutchoven, cook meat, several pieces at a time, until well browned on all sides, Remove pieces as they brown.

To drippings in Dutchoven, add chopped carrot and onion and cook over medium heat, stirring frequently, until tender, about 5 minutes.

Return the beef to Dutchoven; pour brandy over all and set a flame with match. When flaming stops add garlic, salt, thyme, leaves, pepper, bay leave and burgundy. Cover and bake in 325 °F oven 3-1/2 hours or until fork-tender.

About 1 hour before meat is done, in medium skillet over medium heat, in 2 tablespoons hot butter or margarine, sauté mushrooms about 7 minutes. Meanwhile, in small bowl with spoon, mix 2 tablespoons softened butter or margarine and 2 tablespoons flour until smooth.

Remove Dutchoven from oven, into hot liquid in Dutchoven, add flour mixture, 1/2 teaspoon at a time, stirring after each addition, until blended. Add reserved onions and mushrooms to Dutchoven. Cover and bake until onions are fork-tender. Serves 8-10.

## Papillon Kabob-Papyon Kebab

-Turkish-

1 pound flank steak
8 slices Swiss deluxe cheese
2 cups sliced mushrooms

1/8 teaspoon cayenne pepper
Salt and black pepper to taste
2 tablespoons margarine or butter

This is one of the most delicious kinds of kabob in Turkish cuisine. Istanbul's special kabob restaurants often have it in their menus.

Cut flank steaks into square pieces; pound each pieces to 1/4-inch thickness. Place Swiss cheese slices over steak pieces, spoon sliced mushroom in the center of steaks. Roll to make small pockets (burrito fashion). If necessary, fasten them with wooden picks. In large skillet, over medium high heat, place the stuffed meat pockets seam side down. Cook them in hot margarine until all sides are browned. Sprinkle with salt and black and cayenne pepper. Serve hot with rice and salad. Serves 4.

## Shish Kabob-Sis Kebab

*-Turkish-*
*2-pounds tenderloin or lamb cubes*
*2 medium green peppers*
*3 medium onions*
*3 tomatoes*
*1-pound mushroom*

*1 teaspoon mixed spices*
*1/4 teaspoon garlic powder*
*1/2 cup olive oil*
*1/2 small onion, minced*
*1/2 cup lemon juice*
*1/2 teaspoon dried mint (optional)*

Grilled meat techniques are much the same around the world, but nowhere are they better used than in Turkey which is justifiably famous for its shish kabob (Sis kebab). The accumulation of several small details make this one of the most delicious of all shish kabobs. The cut of the meat, the size of the meat pieces, intensity of the heat and speed of cooking together are very important to achieving good results. In this recipe you need to use meat from loin, no other cut will do. The heat must be intense. The meat must be grilled very quickly, thus the juices are sealed in. The marinade is not for tenderizing but for a bold and spicy taste.

Marinade: In large pan, combine mixed spices, garlic powder, olive oil, minced onion, lemon juice and mint. Mix thoroughly. Sprinkle salt over meat cubes and add to the marinade. Mix well, cover and set aside for 1/2 to 1 hour.

1 hour before serving, prepare, the tomato and onion wedges and cut peppers into 2-inch squares. Prepare the outdoor grill or barbecue. On skewers, thread meat cubes alternately with vegetables. Place skewers on barbecue, over medium-high coals. Cook until meat is of desired doneness, turning often and brushing with remaining marinade. Serve with rice pilaf. Serves 6.

## Baked Pot Roast

*1 (3-pound) beef round rump*
*   roast*
*1 large onion, sliced*
*1 garlic clove, crushed*
*2 tablespoons Worcestershire*
*3 teaspoons salt*
*1 teaspoon sugar*

*1/4 teaspoon cracked*
*   black pepper*
*2 cups water*
*4 medium parsnips, cut into*
*   chunks*
*1 (24-ounce) bag frozen lima beans*
*Parsley sprigs for garnish*

In medium Dutchoven, place beef round rump roast. Add onion, garlic, Worcestershire, salt, sugar, pepper and water. Cover and bake in 350 °F oven for 2 hours. Add the parsnip chunks and lima beans to Dutchoven and continue baking 1 to 1-1/2 hours more until vegetables and meat are fork-tender, turning the meat occasionally. Transfer the meat to warm platter. Remove the strings and discard them. With slotted spoon, arrange vegetables around meat. With large spoon, skim fat from the liquid in Dutchoven. Serve liquid over meat and vegetables. Garnish with parsley. Serves 10

# Beef Fajitas

*-Mexican-*
*1 pound beef strips*
*1 green pepper, sliced*
*1 red pepper, sliced*
*1 large onion, sliced*
*2 large tomatoes, chopped*
*1-pound cheddar cheese,*
  *shredded*

*1 (8-ounce) sour cream*
*1 avocado, peeled and diced*
*1 teaspoon Mexican mixed spices*
*1/2 teaspoon salt*
*1/4 teaspoon garlic powder*
*3 tablespoons margarine*

Place chopped tomatoes, avocado and sour cream into separate small serving bowls and place them on the dinner table.

In large skillet over medium-high heat, in hot margarine, cook beef strips. Add sliced onion and peppers season with mixed spices, salt and garlic; cook until beef strips and vegetables are just tender.

Meanwhile heat tortillas in the oven, about 2 to 3 minutes. While they are soft and warm, place on plate. Spoon cooked beef and vegetables in the center of each tortillas, topping with some cheese, tomatoes, avocado, and sour cream. Fold tortillas over the fillings. Serve with Mexican beer and lime wedges if you like. Serves 4.

# Beef Burritos

*-Mexican-*
*1 pound beef for stew, cut into*
  *1/2-inch chunks*
*1 cup chopped onions*
*1 garlic clove, minced*
*1 (16-ounce) can refried beans*
*1/4 teaspoon Mexican mixed*
  *spices*

*1 package ready tortillas*
*Water*
*Salad oil*
*1/2 cup shredded cheddar cheese, melted*
*1 (4-ounce) can diced green chilies*
*1 green onion, minced*

In large skillet over medium-high heat; in 2 tablespoons salad oil, cook beef until browned. Add onion, garlic, 1/2 teaspoon salt, Mexican mixed spices, red pepper and 1-1/2 cups water and heat to boiling. Reduce heat to low, cover and simmer 2 hours, until meat is fork-tender and begins to fall apart.

About 5 minutes before meat mixture is done, in small saucepan over medium heat, in 1 tablespoon hot oil, heat refried beans and 1/4 cup cheese until hot and cheese is melted, stirring occasionally.

When meat is done, add chilies and gently flake meat apart. Continue cooking until mixture is thickened and all liquid is evaporated.

In the center of each tortilla, spread about 2 tablespoons bean mixture in a thin layer. Spoon on about 2 tablespoons meat mixture. Fold tortilla over filling to make a package. Repeat the same process with remaining mixture. Pour melted cheese over the packages before serving, garnish with minced green onion. Serves 8.

# Beef Stroganoff

4 beef chuck top blade
  steaks boneless, each cut
  1-inch thick
1 tablespoon butter
1 medium onion, chopped
1 teaspoon salt
1/4 teaspoon pepper
Water

1 (8-ounce) package wide
  egg noodles
1 tablespoon all-purpose flour
1/2 cup sour cream
1 tablespoon chopped parsley
1 teaspoon mustard
1/2 pound mushrooms, sliced

In large skillet over medium high-heat, in hot butter, cook steaks and onion until meat is well-browned on both sides, about 10 minutes, Add salt, pepper, 1/4 cup water and mustard, heat to boiling: Reduce heat to low, cover and simmer 1-1/4 hours or until steaks are fork-tender.

Add mushrooms and reheat. About 20 minutes before the steaks are done prepare noodles as label directs. Spoon noodles onto warm platter. Arrange steaks and mushrooms on the same platter over the noodles, keep warm.

In small cup stir flour and 1/4 cup water until blended. Gradually stir into liquid in skillet, cook over medium heat until sauce is thickened, stirring; stir in sour cream; heat through (do not boil. Spoon sauce over steaks and noodles. Sprinkle with parsley. Serves 6.

# Ginger Beef

-Cantonese-
2 tablespoons reduced-sodium
  soy sauce
2 tablespoons water
1 tablespoon cornstarch
1/4 teaspoon ground ginger
1/8 teaspoon garlic powder
1 pound beef flank or sirloin
  steak, thinly sliced

2 teaspoons vegetable oil
1 medium green pepper, cut into thin
  strips
1 tomato, cut into wedges
4 green onions, sliced
3 cups rice pilaf (page 111)

In small mixing bowl, blend soy sauce, water, cornstarch, ginger and garlic powder. Add beef and stir to coat. Cover. Marinate for 30 minutes at room temperature. In medium skillet, heat oil over medium-high heat, add green pepper strips and stir-fry for 2 minutes. Add meat mixture. Stir fry until meat is no longer pink, about 4 minutes. Add tomato and green onions. Stir fry until hot, about 1 minute. Serve over rice pilaf. Serves 6.

# Oriental Beef

1 beef chuck shoulder steak
  boneless, cut into
  1-1/2-inch thick
2 tablespoons cornstarch
2 teaspoons anise seed
1/2 teaspoon ground ginger

1 bunch green onions
1/2 cup dry sherry
1/4 cup soy sauce
1 tablespoon sugar
Water

Cut roots off onions and cut onions into 1-inch pieces. In large skillet, place half of the onion pieces; stir in sherry, soy sauce, sugar, anise seed, ground ginger and 1/4 cup water.

Add the steak over high heat, heat to boiling. Reduce heat to low, cover and simmer steak 1-3/4 hours or until fork-tender, turning steak once. When steak is done, remove to platter and keep warm.

In small cup combine 1/4 cup water and cornstarch until blended. Gradually stir cornstarch mixture into liquid in skillet. Cook over medium heat, stirring constantly until thickened. Stir in remaining half of onion pieces. Spoon sauce over steak. Cut steak into thin slices to serve. Serves 6-8.

# London Broil

1 (1-1/2 pound) beef flank steak
Seasoned salt
Seasoned pepper
2 medium tomatoes

Bottled Italian dressing
6 large mushrooms

Preheat broiler. With sharp knife score both sides of the steak. Place on rack in broiling pan. Sprinkle steak with 1/2 teaspoon seasoned salt, 1/8 teaspoon seasoned pepper. Cut tomatoes in half. Brush tomatoes with Italian dressing and arrange, cut side up, around steak. Broil 5 minutes. Meanwhile, wash and slice mushrooms. With tongs, turn steak; sprinkle with 1/2 teaspoon seasoned salt, 1/8 teaspoon seasoned pepper. Arrange mushroom slices in overlapping rows on broiler rack and brush with Italian dressing. Broil steak 5 minutes more for rare or 6 minutes for medium. To check doneness, with knife, make a small cut in the center of meat. Carve thin diagonal slices across width of steak. Serve slices with broiled vegetables. Spoon drippings over if you like. Serves 4.

## Sultan's Favorite-Hünkâr Beğendi

*-Turkish-*

| | |
|---|---|
| 1 pound tenderloin cubes | 1/3 cup all-purpose flour |
| 3 tablespoons margarine | 3 tablespoons margarine |
| 1/4 medium onion, finely shredded | 2-1/2 cups milk |
| 1/2 medium tomatoes, peeled and finely chopped | 1/2 cup shredded Turkish casserie or Swiss cheese |
| 3-1/4 cup water | Salt |
| 1 lemon juiced | Black pepper to taste |
| 4 slim long eggplants | 1 teaspoon sugar |

This is one of the great classic Ottoman dishes. It was originally called "Her majesty's favorite". It is a delicate dish that is not easy to make but well worth trying. The name refers to Empress Eugenie, the wife of Napoleon III, who fell in love with it on her visit to Sultan Abdulaziz.

Meat Kabob: In large saucepan, over medium heat, in 1 tablespoon hot margarine, cook meat cubes until all sides are browned. With slotted spoon remove meat to large plate.

To drippings, add onion cook until tender. Add finely chopped tomatoes, cooked meat cubes, salt to taste, pepper and water. Cover and cook until meat cubes are tender and most of the liquid is absorbed, about 1-1/2 hours.

Eggplant delight: Meanwhile, rinse and pat dry eggplants. Broil until they are soft inside. Remove burned skins, rinse under running cold water. Place them in small bowl, add lemon juice; cover and set aside for 15 minutes. In medium saucepan over medium heat, in 2 tablespoons of hot margarine, cook flour 3 minutes. Remove from heat, mash eggplants in food processor until smooth. Add into flour-margarine mixture.

Return pan to heat, gradually adding milk. Sprinkle with salt, stirring quickly and frequently. Cook until mixture is slightly thickened. Remove from heat and sprinkle with shredded cheese. Reheat meat kabobs; spoon eggplant mixture in the center of plates and top with meat kabobs. Serves 4-6.

## Roast Beef with Wine-Mustard Sauce

*-Swiss-*

| | |
|---|---|
| 3 medium onions, sliced | 1 (5-pounds) beef bottom round roast |
| 3 medium carrots, sliced | 2 tablespoons all-purpose flour |
| 2-1/2 cups dry red wine | 1/4 teaspoon cracked black pepper |
| 2 cups water | Salt |
| 1/4 cup red wine vinegar | 1/4 cup salad oil |
| 2 large celery stalks, sliced | 1/3 cup fine gingersnap crumbs |
| 2 bay leaves | 1/2 cup sour cream |
| 6 peppercorns | |
| 1/4 teaspoon mustard seed | |

In medium saucepan, over medium heat, heat 2 onions, 1 carrot and next 7 ingredients to boiling. Reduce heat to low, cover saucepan and simmer 10 minutes. Pour into large bowl, cover and cool. Add roast, turning to coat. Cover and refrigerate 8 hours, turning the meat occasionally. About 4 hours before serving, remove meat, dry with paper towels, coat with flour, pepper and 1 teaspoon salt. Strain marinade, reserving liquid. In large Dutchoven over medium-high heat, in hot oil, cook meat until browned. Remove meat and pour off all but 1 tablespoon of the drippings. In drippings over medium heat, cook rest of vegetables 3 minutes, stirring. Add meat and marinade, heat to boiling. Reduce heat to low, cover and simmer 3-1/2 hours turning occasionally. Remove meat to warm platter and keep warm. Spoon off and discard the fat from gravy. Add cookie crumbs and 1/2 teaspoon salt. Over medium-high heat, stir until mixture thickens. With wire whisk, blend in sour cream. Cook, stirring constantly until heated through. Serve sour-cream gravy separately. Serves 14.

## Leman's Mediterranean Baby Lamb Chops

8 lamb chops
4 Japanese eggplants
Salt
Pepper
4 medium tomatoes,
  peeled and diced

Minced parsley
1 cup ricotta cheese
2 small garlic cloves, minced
1/4 teaspoon thyme
Butter
2 teaspoons mixed spices

In small bowl add ricotta cheese, parsley, garlic, mixed spices and mix well. Set aside.
Wash eggplants, trim ends, slice into 1/4-inch thick pieces, cut the slices lengthwise making strips (French cut) and set aside.
In small saucepan over medium heat, in 2 tablespoons hot butter, cook eggplant strips until browned.
In large saucepan, in hot 1/2 tablespoon butter; add diced tomatoes, 1/2 teaspoon salt, 1/4 teaspoon thyme, 1/4 teaspoon pepper and cook over medium heat until tomatoes are tender. Place lamb chops on grill, sprinkle with salt and pepper and grill both sides until lamb chops are tender.
Place lamb chops on side of plates and place 1 large scoop of herbed ricotta and 1 large spoonful eggplant strips and tomato mixture on each plate. Serve with toasted French bread. Serves 4.

## Anatolian-Style Cooked lamb and Vegetables-Güveçte Türlü

-Turkish-

6 lamb shoulder
blade chops
18 small new potatoes
peeled
2 large carrots, peeled,
and sliced
1 garlic clove, minced
2 medium zucchinis
1 large tomato, peeled and
cut into chunks

Salt to taste
1 bay leaf
1/2 teaspoon pepper
3 tablespoons margarine
1 tablespoon chopped parsley
1/4 cup port wine (optional)

Many parts of Turkey offer this slow cooked dish as well as similar ones. "Toprak kap, Güveç" means earthenware in Turkish, and "Karisik sebze-Türlü" means mixed vegetables. A large earthenware casserole is filled with meat, usually lamb, plus every kind of vegetable imaginable then and cooked slowly.

In large earthenware cooking pot, over medium heat, in melted margarine, cook chopped onions until tender. Add lamb, cook stirring until lamb is browned.

Add water to cover the lamb, add salt, pepper, minced garlic, parsley, wine and bay leaf; cover and reduce the heat medium-low and cook until meat is tender. Then add potato chunks, sliced carrots, peeled tomato wedges and cook until vegetables are tender. Add zucchini slices in the last 15 minutes of cooking time. Discard bay leaf, serve hot. Serves 4.

## Slow Roasted Leg of Lamb-Firinda Kuzu Budu

-Turkish-

1 (5-pound) whole lamb leg
1/4 teaspoon black pepper
1 teaspoon salt
2 teaspoons Grey Poupon mustard
Water
Wine-Red Currant Sauce (optional):
1/2 cup red currant jelly
2 tablespoons cornstarch
Water
1/4 cup cooking wine

Garnishing (optional):
Parsley, finely minced,
sumac and sliced red onion

Mix mustard, pepper, 1 teaspoon salt and 2 teaspoons water, brush lamb with this mixture. Place lamb on rack roasting pan, add 1 cup water and roast 1 hour in 350 °F oven basting occasionally with pan dripping. Reduce heat to 325 °F and cover lamb leg with aluminum foil roasting for 3 to 3-1/2 hours more until well done. Remove excess fat.

If you prefer separate meat into flakes and serve over pilaf. Garnish with minced parsley, sliced red onion and sumac.

Or if you prefer, serve with wine and red currant sauce: Pour remaining pan liquid in small saucepan, add 1-1/4 cups water. Cook over medium heat, stirring to loosen the bits. Add wine. Add water to make 1-3/4 cups and red currant jelly, heat to boiling, stirring constantly until the jelly is melted. Blend cornstarch, 1/4 teaspoon salt and 1/4 cup water and stir into liquid in saucepan until thickened. Carve lamb and serve sauce separately. Serve with rice pilaf with raisins and almonds. Garnish pilaf with minced parsley. Serves 12.

## Marinated Leg of Lamb from Barcelona

*-Spanish-*
*1/2 cup orange juice*
*1/2 cup dry red wine*
*1/2 cup chili sauce*
*2 tablespoons salad oil*
*1 small onion, minced*
*1 garlic clove minced*
*1 tablespoons sugar*
*Salt*

*2 teaspoons chili powder*
*1 teaspoon basil*
*1 (4-pound) lamb leg shank half*
*Water*
*3 tablespoons all-purpose flour*

In large shallow pan, mix 1 teaspoon salt and remaining ingredients except leg of lamb, water and flour. Add lamb and turn over to coat with marinade. Cover with plastic wrap and refrigerate at least 12 hours, turning lamb occasionally. About 3-1/2 hours before serving, place lamb, fat side up, on rack in open roasting pan. Reserve marinade. Insert meat thermometer into center of meat, being careful thermometer does not touch bone. Roast in 325 °F oven about 1-2/3 hours or until meat thermometer reaches 140 °F for rare, 160 °F for medium or 170 °F for well done, basting occasionally with marinade. Place meat on warm platter and let rest 15 minutes. Meanwhile, make gravy: Pour pan liquid into a 4 cup measure or medium bowl (set pan aside), let stand a few minutes until fat separates from meat liquid. Skim 3 tablespoons fat from liquid into 2-quart saucepan; skim remaining fat and discard. Add 1-1/2 cups water to roasting pan; cook over medium heat, stirring until brown bits are loosened. Add mixture and reserved marinade to liquid in small cup. (Add more water if needed to make 2-1/2 cups). Over medium heat, into hot fat in saucepan, stir flour and 1/4 teaspoon salt until blended. Gradually stir in liquid mixture and cook, stirring until thickened. Serve gravy with lamb. Serves 10.

## Navarin of Lamb

*-Mediterranean-*
*1-1/2 oz. all-purpose flour*
*1 teaspoon salt*
*1/2 teaspoon white pepper*
*2 pounds best-end of neck*
 *lamb chops*
*2 tablespoons cooking oil*
*1 onion sliced*
*1/2 pounds carrots, peeled*
 *and cut into thick strips*

*2 small turnips peeled and cut into cubes*
*1 pint chicken stock*
*2 tablespoons tomato puree*
*1 teaspoon rosemary*
*6 oz. button onions, peeled*

Preheat oven to 350 °F. Mix together flour, salt and pepper. Trim fat from chops and dust in the seasoned flour. Fry in the oil for three minutes on each side and place in ovenproof casserole. Reserve remaining flour mixture. Fry the onion until beginning to soften, then add carrots, turnips, and remaining flour. Continue to fry gently for two minutes. Gradually add the stock and tomato puree, stirring continuously until the sauce boils. Add rosemary and pour into casserole with the chops. Place in the oven and cook for 2 hours, adding the button onions 30 minutes before the end of the cooking time. If button onions are unobtainable, use larger onions and cut into quarters before adding to casserole. Serves 6.

## Veal Rump Roast

*1 (4-pound) veal leg rump*
 *roast boneless*
*3 medium carrots, diced*
*1 medium onion, chopped*
*2/3 cup water*
*1 (10-3/4 ounce) can condensed*
 *cream of mushroom soup*

*1 teaspoon salt*
*1/4 teaspoon cracked*
 *black pepper corns*
*1/4 teaspoon marjoram leaves*
*1 bay leaf*

In large Dutchoven, over medium-high heat, cook veal leg rump roast until well browned on all sides. Push roast to one side of the Dutchoven, add carrots and onion. Cook, stirring occasionally, about 5 minutes. Remove any excess fat.

Add water, soup, salt, pepper, Majoram leaves and bay leaf; heat to boiling, stirring constantly. Reduce heat to low; cover and simmer 2-1/2 to 3 hours until meat is fork-tender. Place meat on warm platter and discard bay leaf. Pour pan liquid into gravy boat, serve separately. Serves 8-12.

# Lemon Tarragon Veal Roast By the Lac Leman

2 teaspoons salt
2 teaspoons grated lemon
  peel
1 teaspoon tarragon leaves
1 (4-pound) veal shoulder roast
  boneless

Water
1/4 cup all-purpose flour
1 beef-flavor bouillon cube

In small bowl, stir together salt, grated lemon peel and tarragon leaves. With tip of sharp knife, make about 2 dozen slits, about 2-1/2-inches deep, over top and sides of veal shoulder roast, taking care not to cut string. Into each slit in the meat, with spoon, insert some of salt mixture. Sprinkle any remaining salt mixture over veal roast. Place meat on rack in open roasting pan, insert meat thermometer into center of thickest part of meat. Roast in 325 °F oven 2-3/4 hours or until temperature is 170 °F. Place veal on warm platter; let stand 15 minutes for easier carving. With knife, carefully remove strings. Meanwhile, prepare the gravy. Spoon off any fat from drippings in roasting pan. Add 1-1/2 cups water to drippings, stir to loosen brown bits at the bottom of the pan. In cup, blend flour with 1/2 cup water until smooth; gradually stir into liquid in roasting pan. Stir in the bouillon cube. Cook over medium heat, stirring constantly until the gravy is smooth and thickened. Serve over the meat. Serves 12.

## Veal Chops in Avocado

4 veal chops, 3/4-inch thick
2 tablespoons butter
1/4 pound mushrooms,
  sliced
1/4 cup minced onion
2 tablespoons medium
  sherry
3/4 teaspoon salt

Dash hot pepper sauce
1 small ripe avocado
2 teaspoons cornstarch
1/2 cup heavy or whipping
  cream
1 teaspoon chopped fresh dill

Preheat oven to 350 °F. Slash fat on edge of chops. In large skillet with oven safe handle, over medium heat, in hot butter, cook mushrooms and onion until tender, about 5 minutes. Arrange chops in skillet. Add sherry, salt and hot pepper sauce; heat to boiling. Cover and bake 1 hour or until meat is fork-tender. Cut avocado in half, remove seed and skin. Slice avocado and arrange over chops. Bake, uncovered, 10 minutes or until avocado is heated through. Place chops on warm platter. Blend cornstarch and 1 tablespoon cream until smooth; stir in remaining cream. Gradually stir into hot liquid in skillet and cook over medium heat, stirring until thickened. Stir in dill. Serve chops immediately with sauce. Serves 4.

## Schnitzel

*-German-*
*6 large veal cutlets*
*2 eggs*
*1 teaspoon salt*
*1/3 cup all-purpose flour*
*1/2 cup margarine*

*2 lemons cut into 8 wedges*
*3 tablespoons chopped parsley*
*1/2 teaspoon coarsely ground*
  *black pepper*
*1-1/2 cups dried bread crumbs*

With meat mallet, pound veal cutlets to about 1/4-inch thickness, turning once. In large bowl beat eggs and add salt and pepper. On waxed paper, place flour; on another sheet, place bread crumbs. Coat veals in flour, then dip in eggs, then well coat with bread crumbs. In large skillet over medium heat, in 1/4 cup hot margarine, cook veals, a few pieces at a time, 3 or 4 minutes on each side until browned, adding margarine as needed. Remove to platter. Garnish with lemon wedges. Serve with winter salad. Serves 6.

## Pagliacci's Veal Rib Chops

*-California style-*
*6 veal rib chops, each*
  *1/2-inch thick*
*1/4 cup all-purpose flour*
*Butter or margarine*
*1 garlic clove, halved*

*1/2 pound mushrooms,*
  *thinly sliced*
*1/2 cup dry vermouth*
*1 teaspoon salt*
*1/8 teaspoon pepper*

On waxed pepper, coat chops lightly with flour. In large skillet over medium-high heat, in 2 tablespoons hot butter, cook garlic until brown. Discard garlic. In butter remaining in skillet, cook chops, half at a time until well browned on both sides. Remove chops as they brown to platter adding a little more butter to skillet if needed. Reduce heat to low. In the same skillet, melt 2 tablespoons more butter and cook mushrooms until just tender. Stir in vermouth, salt and pepper, scraping to loosen brown bits. Return chops to skillet. Cover and simmer 15 minutes until chops are fork-tender. To serve, arrange chops on warm platter and pour mushroom mixture over chops. Serves 6.

## Milanese

4 veal cutlets, 1/4-inch thick
1/4 cup butter
1/4 cup medium sherry

1/4 pound thinly sliced
  prosciutto ham, cut in thin
  strips
1/2 pound raclette cheese

Preheat oven to 350 °F. With meat mallet, pound cutlets until about 1/8-inch thick, turning once. In large skillet over medium-high heat, in hot butter, cook cutlets until lightly browned on both sides. Place in 12x8-inch baking dish. To drippings in skillet, add sherry and stir to loosen brown bits; pour over meat. Arrange prosciutto strips over veal. Bake 5 minutes. Remove from oven; coarsely shred raclette cheese and sprinkle over. Bake 4 to 5 minutes more until cheese is melted. Serves 4.

## Boiled Beef Tongue

2 pounds beef tongue
2 medium onions
2 large tomatoes, diced
1 small sweet green pepper
1 carrot, peeled
1 tablespoon all-purpose
  flour
2-1/2 cups diluted beef broth

2 bay leaves
1/2 bunch parsley, minced
2 table spoons salad oil
Red wine vinegar
Pepper
Salt

In medium Dutchoven, over high heat, boil water, tongue, 1/2 tablespoon vinegar, bay leaf, pepper and 1 whole peeled onion. Reduce heat to low; cover and simmer until tongue is fork-tender.

In small saucepan, over medium heat, in hot margarine, sauté onions, carrots and half of the minced parsley until onion is tender. Stir in beef broth, diced tomatoes and flour. Add beef broth mixture to onion-carrot sauté. Meanwhile, plunge tongue into cold water, remove skin and cut into thin slices. Cook in the prepared mix for 10 more minutes. Garnish with parsley. Serves to: 8-10

## Liver Pane

-French-
1 large beef liver
2 eggs, beaten
1-1/3 cups all-purpose flour
Salt
Pepper

1/2 cup olive oil
1/2 cup shredded Swiss cheese
1/2 bunch parsley, minced
1 cup dried bread crumbs

Wash liver, pat dry and remove the translucent skin. Cut into 1/4-inch slices. Sprinkle with salt, pepper and shredded cheese, coat with flour then dip in beaten eggs, then coat with bread crumbs.

In large skillet over medium heat, in hot oil, cook panes until golden crisp and liver slices are fork-tender. Serve as a side dish. Garnish with minced parsley. Serves 4.

## Sautéed Lamb Kidneys

-Turkish-
2-pound lamb kidneys
2 medium onions
2 medium tomatoes, peeled
  and diced
1 small sweet green
  pepper, chopped

1-1/2 tablespoons margarine
Pepper
Salt
1 bunch parsley, minced

Remove membranes from kidneys, split kidneys lengthwise and remove white pieces and vein. Rinse under running cold water. Cut each half piece into 4 pieces.

Slice onion. In medium skillet, over medium heat, sauté onions and kidney pieces. Add green pepper, tomatoes, salt and pepper. Cook until kidneys are tender. Garnish with parsley and serve with toasted bread. Sautéed lamb kidneys are served as a side dish. Serves 6.

# SEA FOOD

## Rocky Mountain Trout

2 white onions, thinly sliced
1/3 cup yellow corn meal
1/4 teaspoon pepper
4-6 lemon wedges
2 teaspoons chopped parsley

4 (8-ounce) trout or smelts, cleaned
1 teaspoon salt
1/3 cup all-purpose flour
2 medium tomatoes cut into wedges
Oil for pan-frying

In large skillet over medium heat, sauté onion rings with parsley until soft and translucent. Remove from skillet and set aside.

In shallow dish combine cornmeal, flour, salt and pepper. Rinse trout and shake dry. Dip rinsed trout in cornmeal mixture, thoroughly coating both sides. Over medium-high heat, in hot oil, pan-fry coated trouts 6 to 8 minutes, turning once, until coating is crisp and fish fillets are done.

Spoon sautéed onions around the fish. Serve with lemon and tomato wedges and tarragon salad. Serves 4.

## Fish Steaks with Rosemary

4 (6-ounce) sword fish, grouper
    or sea trout
2 garlic cloves, minced
2 to 4 tablespoons all-purpose
    flour
3 tablespoons olive oil
Salt and pepper to taste

1 teaspoon chopped rosemary
    or 1/4 teaspoon dried leaf rosemary
2 tablespoons white wine vinegar
2 tablespoons water
Pinch of sugar

Rinse fish and pat dry with paper towels. Season with salt and pepper; dust lightly with flour. In large skillet heat oil; place coated fish. Pan-fry fish 3 to 4 minutes on each side until browned and well done, turning once. Arrange fish on platter; keep warm by covering with foil. Add garlic to skillet; sauté 1 minute. Add rosemary, vinegar, water and sugar. Stirring and scraping up bits from skillet, cook sauce until slightly reduced. Spoon sauce over fish; serve immediately. Serves 4.

## Baked Fillets of Sole

8 sole or other fillets
5 tablespoons butter
2 teaspoons salt
1/2 teaspoon lemon juice
1/4 teaspoon pepper

3 tablespoons all-purpose flour
1 cup grated cheddar cheese
3 tablespoons white wine
1-1/4 cups milk
Paprika

Preheat oven to 350 °F. In small saucepan, melt 2 tablespoons butter; brush over sole fillets, sprinkle with salt, lemon juice and pepper.

Roll up each fillet and place open ends down in baking dish. Pour 1/2 cup milk over fillets; bake in oven 25 minutes or until fish flakes easily when tested with fork.

Meanwhile, in small saucepan over medium heat, melt remaining butter, Stir in flour; gradually add remaining milk; cook, stirring, until thickened. Reduce heat; stir in cheese and white wine. Spoon liquid from cooked fish. Stir 1/4 cup liquid into cheese sauce. Pour cheese sauce over fish sprinkle with paprika. Broil about 1 minute, just until cheese sauce is slightly golden. Serves 8.

## Oktay's Marmara Style Halibut-Balik Bugulama

-Turkish-
4 halibut steaks
1 garlic cloves, sliced
2 large tomatoes, peeled
  cut into wedges
2 medium onions, peeled
1 green pepper, sliced into rings
1 tablespoons lemon juice

3 tablespoons olive oil
1 to 2 bay leaves
1/4 teaspoon mixed spices
Salt
Pepper
2 teaspoons chopped parsley

If it is available, you can use The Mediterranean fish "Karagöz" from The Aegean sea or "Levrek" from The Marmara sea (Sea between The Aegean and Black seas).

Rinse and pat dry fish steaks, coat with mixed spices and pepper. In large shallow earthenware cooking dish (heatproof), over medium heat, cook onion rings for 2 minutes.

Arrange halibut steaks on the dish. Reduce heat to over low-medium heat. Arrange tomatoes wedges between steaks, add sliced garlic clove. Place onion rings and bay leaves over the steaks. Sprinkle with parsley, salt and lemon juice. Cover and cook until fish steaks are done. Discard bay leaves. Serves 4.

## Sole Thermidor from Sunset Boulevard

5 tablespoons butter
8 sole or other fillets
2 tablespoons salt
1/2 teaspoon seasoned salt
1/8 teaspoon pepper
1-1/4 cups milk

3 tablespoons all-purpose flour
1 cup grated cheddar cheese
3 tablespoons sherry (optional)
Paprika

Preheat oven to 350 °F. In 1-quart saucepan, melt 2 tablespoons butter; brush over the sole fillets. Sprinkle with salt, seasoned salt and pepper. Roll up each fillet and place seam side down, in 9x9-inch baking dish. Pour 1/2 cup milk over fillets; bake in oven 25 minutes or until fish flakes easily when tested with fork. Meanwhile, in 2-quart saucepan over medium heat, melt remaining butter. Stir in flour; gradually add remaining milk; cook, stirring, until thickened. Reduce heat; stir in cheese and sherry. Preheat broiler. Spoon liquid from cooked fish. Stir 1/4 cup liquid into cheese sauce. (If not using sherry use extra 3 tablespoons liquid). Pour cheese sauce over fish; sprinkle with paprika. Broil about 1 minute, until just cheese sauce is slightly golden. Serves 8.

## Tarragon Flavored Sword Fish Steaks

2 (1-1/2 pound) sword fish or
   halibut steaks
1/3 cup salad oil
1/3 cup tarragon or cider vinegar
2 bay leaves
2 tablespoons chopped parsley

2 teaspoons salt
1 teaspoon Worcestershire
1/4 teaspoon chopped tarragon or 3/4
   teaspoon chopped fresh tarragon
1/ 4 teaspoon pepper
1 lemon

Place fish steaks in large shallow dish. In small bowl combine oil, vinegar, bay leaves, parsley, salt, Worcestershire, tarragon and pepper for marinade; pour over fish, Cover dish and refrigerate for 1/2 hour, turning the fish occasionally to coat in marinade.

Preheat the broiler. Place fish steaks in broiling pan; reserve marinade. And broil 15 minutes or until fish flakes easily when tested with a fork. Baste fish steaks occasionally with marinade.

With pancake turner, carefully lift fish steaks to warm platter. Serve with lemon wedges. Serves 6.

## Grilled Sword Fish

4 (5 to 7-ounce) sword fish
1/4 cup butter or margarine
Salt and pepper to taste

2 small garlic cloves, minced
2 tablespoons finely chopped mint
2 teaspoons lemon juice

Preheat grill; grease rack. Rinse fish; pat dry with paper towels; season with salt and pepper. Melt butter or margarine in small saucepan. Add garlic, chopped mint and lemon juice.

Spoon garlic mixture over seasoned fish. Place on greased rack 3 to 4-inches above hot coals or high heat. Turning once and basting 2 to 3 times with garlic mixture. Grill 5 to 8 minutes or until fish is done. Spoon any remaining garlic mixture over cooked fish. Place fish on platter. Garnish with mint sprigs and lemon slices. Serves 4.


## Fillet of Sole Monterey

6 fillets, 6 oz. each
3 eggs, beaten
1 cup flour
6 ounce bay shrimp
6 ounce tomatoes, diced
6 ounce fresh mushrooms,
  sliced

1 medium shallot, chopped
2 garlic cloves
1/2 lemon
1 tablespoon fresh basil, chopped
5 tablespoons butter
Salt and pepper to taste

Coat fish fillets with flour, then with egg and sauté in 3 tablespoons butter about 3 minutes on each side or until golden brown on both sides. Place on heated platter.

Add remaining butter to pan. Sauté garlic cloves, chopped shallot, mushrooms, tomatoes and basil. Cook one minute. Add bay shrimp, salt and pepper to taste. Place mixture on top of fish and serve. Serves 6.

## Mahi Mahi from Kaanapali

-Hawaiian-
4 fillets Mahi Mahi
2 tablespoons butter
1 tablespoon sugar
1/8 teaspoon red pepper flakes
  crushed

1 cup finely chopped fresh
  pineapple
1/4 cup chopped pecans

Grill fish fillets 3 minutes each side. Reserve on warm platter. Melt butter in skillet over high heat. Add pepper flakes and pecans. Sauté until golden. Add sugar and brown slightly. Add pineapple; sauté until slightly thickened. Spoon over fish fillets. Serves 4.

## Orange Roughy au Gratin

4 fillets, 1/2-pound each
12 tablespoons butter
4 tablespoons chopped fresh
  parsley
4 scallions, white parts
  only, chopped

2 cups chopped fresh
  mushrooms
White pepper
Salt
1/2 cup dry white wine
1/2 cup bread crumbs

Butter large gratin dish and sprinkle the base with half of the parsley, scallions and mushrooms. Season with salt and pepper and lay fish on top.

Cover fish fillets with rest of the chopped ingredients and top with bread crumbs. Add wine, melt remaining butter and sprinkle it over top. Bake in pre-heated 425 °F oven for approximately 10 minutes or until fish is cooked and the top is crisp and golden. At the end of cooking, the fish may be broiled quickly if necessary to color the top. Serves 4.

## Plaice Velouté

*-French-*
*4 large plaice fillets*
*1 tablespoon cooking oil*
*1 small onion, finely chopped*
*2 tomatoes, skinned and*
*    chopped*
*6-oz. peeled prawns*
*1-1/2-oz. fresh white bread*
*    crumbs*

*2-oz. margarine*
*2-oz. plain flour*
*1 pint milk*
*1 tablespoon dried dill*
*5 tablespoons half and half*
*Salt and white pepper to taste*

Preheat oven to 375 °F. Skin the fish. Heat the oil in large saucepan and gently sauté the onion until soft. Add tomatoes and prawns and cook for 1 minute. Stir in bread crumbs. Season with salt and white pepper to taste. Spread this mixture carefully over the fish fillets and gently roll up each one. Place in a shallow oven proof dish.

Melt the butter in large saucepan. Stir in the flour and cook over low heat for 2 minutes, stirring. Gradually blend in the milk and bring to a boil. Add dill, cream, salt and white pepper to taste. Stir well; pour over the fish, cover and cook in oven for 20 minutes. Transfer to serving dish and garnish as desired. Serves 4.

## Salmon Steaks at the Oceanview

*6 salmon steaks*
*1 tablespoon lemon juice*
*Salt and black pepper*
*1/2 cup finely shredded*
*    gruyère or cheddar cheese*
*    (optional)*

*1/4 cup chopped green onions*
*2 tablespoons finely chopped parsley*
*1 tablespoon finely chopped dill or*
*    1/4 bunch dill sprigs*
*1/8 teaspoon red pepper*
*2 tablespoons white vine (optional)*
*Lemon wedges*

Arrange salmon steaks on greased pan. Sprinkle with lemon juice and season lightly with salt and black pepper. Grill fish steaks 6 to 8 minutes or until steaks are done. While grilling, add white wine. Sprinkle with cheese, green onions, parsley, dill, salt and red pepper. Cover and wait 3 minutes to melt cheese and blend the herbs. Serve with lemon wedges and vegetables. Serves 6.

# Poached Halibut with Shrimp Sauce

2 large halibut steaks
1/3 pound small shrimp
4 large green onions
3 sprigs parsley
1/2 cup dry white wine
3 cups water

2 tablespoons unsalted butter
2 cloves garlic, minced
1/8 teaspoon paprika
1/8 teaspoon cayenne pepper
1/2 cup whipping cream
Salt and white or cayenne
    pepper to taste

Bone and skin halibut steaks and peel and devein shrimp. Thinly slice white parts of green onions and set aside; cut green tops into 1-inch pieces. Combine the halibut bones and skin, shrimp shell, green onion tops, and parsley in saucepan. Add wine and water to cover. Bring to a boil, reduce to a simmer, and cook 30 minutes, skimming off any foam that rises to surface. Keep at a simmer.

In medium skillet, over medium heat, melt butter. Add garlic, reserved green onions, paprika, and cayenne pepper and cook until onions soften. Add shrimp and cook until turn opaque. Meanwhile, in a lightly oiled deep skillet arrange halibut steaks. Strain hot stock over fish, adding boiling water if necessary to cover fish with liquid. Bring to a simmer, over low heat; do not boil. Poach fish until desired doneness. To prevent fish from overcooking and becoming dry, remove it when the very center still offers a little resistance. Fish will continue cooking from heat on the surface. If the shrimps gets done before the halibut, remove them from heat.

Remove poached halibut steaks with slotted spatula, drain them thoroughly, and place them in oven proof pan. Keep warm in a low oven.

Bring the poaching liquid to a rolling boil until flecks of albumin (like egg whites) congeal on top. Strain through a fine sieve to remove the albumin, and add 1 cup of strained liquid to shrimp skillet. Bring to a boil and reduce by half. Stir in cream and reduce by half again. While the sauce is reducing, carefully pour the juices that have accumulated on the halibut platter back into the sauce and blot away any remaining liquid with paper towel. Season the sauce to taste and pour it over halibut and shrimp. Surround fish with a colorful assortment of julienned vegetables. Serves 4.

## Spanish Fish Stew

*-Spanish-*
*3 tablespoons olive oil*
*1 large onion, chopped*
*3 garlic cloves, minced*
*1/2 cup diced green bell pepper*
*1 (16-oz.) can whole peeled*
*  tomatoes undrained, chopped*
*2 (8-oz.) bottles clam juice*
*2-3/4 cups water*
*2 tablespoons tomato paste*
*1 bay leaf*
*1/2 teaspoon ground turmeric*

*1 teaspoon finely chopped thyme*
*  or 1/2 teaspoon dried leaf thyme*
*1/4 teaspoon crushed fennel seeds*
*1/8 teaspoon sugar*
*1/8 teaspoon saffron powder*
*Salt*
*Ground black pepper*
*1-1/2 pound skinless firm-texture fish*
*  fillets*
*12 to 18 peeled, deveined medium*
*  shrimp*

In large kettle over medium heat, sauté onion, garlic and green pepper until onion is soft and translucent. Add tomatoes and liquid, clam juice, water, tomato paste, bay leaf, turmeric, thyme, fennel seeds, sugar and saffron, if desired. Cover and simmer 15 minutes. Add salt and black pepper to taste. Cut fish into 1-inch pieces. Add fish pieces and shrimp to soup. Simmer gently 4 to 5 minutes or until fish becomes firm and turns opaque and shrimp becomes firm and turns pink. Remove and discard bay leaf. Spoon stew into medium tureen or serve in individual bowls. Serves 6.

## Fried Cod Fillets

*Vegetable oil for deep frying*
*1 cup all-purpose flour*
*1/2 teaspoon salt*
*2 (16-ounce) cod or other fillets*
*1/2 teaspoon salt*

*1/2 teaspoons baking powder*
*1 egg*
*1 cup milk*
*Lemon wedges*
*Cider vinegar*

Cut fish into 2-inch pieces; pat fish dry with paper towels. In medium bowl, combine flour, salt, dill, baking powder, egg and milk. Beat with fork until smooth. Dip fish pieces into batter; let excess batter drip back into bowl.

Fry 4 to 5 coated fish pieces at a time, 3 to 5 minutes or until golden brown. Drain on paper towels. Keep warm in oven until all pieces are cooked. Arrange fried fish on large platter. If you like serve with fried potatoes, lemon wedges and your choice of fresh salad. Serves 6-8.

## Fish Fillets in Havarti Sauce

-California style-

1-1/2 pound skinless and dab,
 sole, pompano or other
 lean white fish fillets
Salt and mixed spices
White pepper
1/2 lemon, juiced
1 egg yolk

1/3 cup milk
4 oz. Danish Havarti cheese,
 shredded
2 teaspoons finely chopped fresh dill
Dill sprigs or dried dill

Preheat oven to 450 °F. Gently rinse fillets; pat dry with paper towels. Season with salt, mixed spices and white pepper; sprinkle with lemon juice. Cut seasoned fillets into 20 strips, 5 to 6 inches long and 1 to 1-1/2 inches wide. Roll up each strip like a pinwheels. Place in a single layer in oiled dish, fasten the seamsides with wooden picks; set aside. In top of double boiler, beat egg yolk and 1/3 cup milk until blended. Place over simmering water and cook, stirring constantly, until mixture thickens enough to coat spoon. Add cheese and dill; continue to cook and stir until cheese is melted. Cover surface of sauce with waxed paper; set aside. Bake fish pinwheels 5 to 8 minutes or until fish is done; drain on paper towels. Reserve fish juices in dish. Carefully remove wooden picks from cooked fish. Arrange 5 pinwheels on each of 4 warm plates. Reheat cheese sauce with more liquid or milk, if necessary. Spoon sauce over and around pinwheels. Garnish with dill sprigs. Serves 4.


## Herbed Pepper Red Snapper

1 chicken bouillon cube
2 small yellow, green and red
 sweet peppers, chopped
1/3 cup sliced green onions
Rice pilaf (page 111)
Orange slices

2 tablespoons grated parmesan cheese
1 pound fresh red snapper fillets
1 tablespoon margarine or butter
1 teaspoon lemon juice
Sliced green onion tops
1/8 teaspoon black and red pepper
 mixture

Prepare rice pilaf as in page 111. While preparing rice pilaf, add chicken bouillon cube into water. Remove from heat; cover; let stand 5 minutes. Stir in peppers, onions, and parmesan cheese.

Spread rice pilaf mixture in greased baking dish. Arrange fish on top. In saucepan melt margarine; stir in lemon juice, 1/8 teaspoon black and red pepper mixture; drizzle over fish. Cover and bake in 350 °F oven 25 to 30 minutes. Garnish with onion tops and orange. Serves 4.

## Santa Monica's Fish and Chips

*-California style-*
*5 medium potatoes, peeled*
*1-1/2 lb. skinless cod or*
  *other firm texture fillets*
*Vegetable oil for deep frying*
*1 cup all purpose flour*
*1/2 teaspoon salt*

*1/2 teaspoon baking powder*
*1 egg*
*1 cup milk*
*Lemon wedges*
*Cider vinegar*
*Salt*

Cut potatoes lengthwise in 1/2-inch thick French-fry strips; set aside. Cut fish in 1-1/2 to 2-inch pieces; set aside. In deep-fat fryer or heavy saucepan, heat oil to 365 °F or hot enough that a 1-inch cube of bread turns golden brown in 1 minute. Cut potatoes into strips. Preheat oven to 165 °F. Fill medium wire frying basket one-fourth full with potato strips. Slowly lower basket into hot oil. If oil bubbles excessively, raise and lower basket several times. Deep fry potatoes 5 to 7 minutes or until golden. Drain potatoes on paper towels, then arrange on large baking sheet. Heat oil again to 365 °F. Fry remaining potatoes in 3 batches; remove basket; do not use basket for frying fish.

Pat fish dry with paper towels. In medium bowl, combine flour, salt, baking powder, egg and milk. Beat with fork until smooth. Dip fish into batter; let excess batter drip back into bowl. Fry 4 or 5 coated fish pieces at a time, 3 to 5 minutes or until golden brown. Drain on paper towels. Keep warm in oven until all pieces are cooked; remove fish from oven. Broil potatoes, 6 inches from the heat, 2 to 3 minutes or until crisp. Arrange fried fish and chips on large platter; garnish with lemon wedges. Serve with vinegar and sprinkle fish and chips with salt. Serves 4-6.

## Boiled Lobster

*Water*
*4 (1-pound) live Maine lobster*
  *or other large lobster*

*Butter, melted*
*Lemon wedges*
*Mayonnaise*

Pour water 6 to 8 inches deep into large kettle. Cover kettle; bring water to a boil. Grasp a lobster firmly behind the head; plunge head first into boiling water. Partially cover the kettle; bring water back to simmer. Begin timing when water begins to simmer. Cook 1-pound lobster 6 to 8 minutes. Add 2 to 3 minutes for each additional pound. Use tongs to remove cooked lobsters from kettle; drain on paper towels. Repeat with remaining lobster. Serve cooked lobster warm with butter or margarine and lemon wedges. Or chill cooked lobsters in their shells; serve with mayonnaise. Provide quests with small forks and pincers to crack shells. Serves 4.

# Grilled Lobster Tails from Mersin

*-Turkish-*
*Lemon-Garlic-Butter Sauce:*
*1/2 cup butter or margarine*
*1 garlic clove, finely chopped*
*1 teaspoon finely shredded*
  *lemon peel*
*2 tablespoons lemon juice*
*1/2 teaspoon finely chopped chives*
  *or green onion tops*

*4 (1/2-lb) lobster tails*
*Lemon wedges*

Mersin is a lovely city on the southern coast of Turkey. Lemon-Garlic-Butter Sauce: Melt butter or margarine in small saucepan; stir in remaining ingredients to taste. Preheat grill. To prepare lobster, cut along edges of tail undershells with kitchen shears. Clip off fins along outer edges. Peel back and discard soft undershell. Bend tail backward, cracking several joints in overshell to prevent curling. Brush lobster with Lemon-Garlic-Butter Sauce. Grease rack; place lobster, shellside down, on greased rack 4 to 6 inches above hot coals or high heat. Cover grill with lid or foil; cut 2 slits in center of foil for vents. Or, cover lobster with a tent of heavy foil. Grill 5 minutes. Brush again with sauce. Turn lobster. Cover and cook 3 to 5 minutes longer or until flesh is opaque. Serve with remaining sauce. Garnish with lemon wedges. If you like you can serve lobster tails with fresh Mediterranean salad. Serves 4.

# Oktay's Oven-Baked Shrimp with Cheese-Karides Güveç

*-Turkish-*
*1 pound shrimp, deveined*
*1 medium onion, peeled*
*2 medium tomatoes peeled and*
  *chopped*
*1 each medium green, red and*
  *yellow bell peppers, chopped*
*1 cup sliced mushrooms*
*2 cups water*

*3/4 cup shredded Turkish casserie*
  *or Swiss cheese*
*Butter or margarine*
*Salt to taste*
*1/2 teaspoon black pepper*
*1/2 teaspoon mixed spices*
*2 tablespoons lemon juice*
*1 tablespoon chopped fresh parsley*

This Turkish dish is usually served as a starter; a fresh fish dish follows later. Melt butter in large earthenware cooking pot. Add sliced onion rings, cook 5 minutes, add tomatoes; cook for 5 minutes. Add rest of the ingredients and water, except shrimp; cook until vegetables reached desired doneness. Remove from heat; add shrimps.

Place pot in 350 °F oven and bake until shrimps are done. 5 to 7 minutes before removing pot from oven; sprinkle with shredded cheese and cayenne pepper.

Serve immediately. You can also cook this dish in 4 separate small earthenware cooking dishes. Serves 4.

## Leman's Jumbo Shrimp Cocktail from Istanbul

*Shrimp Cocktail Sauce:*
*1/2 cup ketchup*
*1 tablespoon minced green onion*
  *or chives*
*1 tablespoon lemon juice*
*1 dash liquid hot pepper sauce*
*1 cup mayonnaise*
*1/8 teaspoon sugar*

*4 red-leaf or butter lettuce leaves*
*1 cup shredded lettuce*
*1/2 cup cocktail sauce*
*16 jumbo shrimps, steamed,*
  *chilled and peeled,*
  *tail shells left on*
*4 lemon wedges*

Cocktail Sauce: Combine all ingredients. Let stand at least 15 minutes for flavors to combine.

Prepare 4 shallow stemmed glasses (champagne or oversized Margarita glasses are traditional) with lettuce leaves, tearing each leaf open at the stem end and overlapping the lower parts to make the leaf as nearly circular possible. Pile shredded lettuce in the center of each glass and top with cocktail sauce. Hang 4 shrimps around edge of each glass. Notch lemon wedges and fix 1 to edge of each glass. Serves 4.

## Shrimp Rémoulade

*Rémoulade Sauce:*
*1/4 cup finely chopped green onions*
*1/4 cup chopped parsley*
*2 tablespoons canned pimento*
*3 tablespoons dijon style mustard*
*2 tablespoons tarragon vinegar*
*1 tablespoon prepared horseradish*
*1/2 cup mayonnaise*
*1 teaspoon paprika*
*1/4 teaspoon cayenne pepper*
*Dash of Worcestershire*
*1/4 teaspoon salt*

*4 large and 4 small leaves butter lettuce*
*1 cup Rémoulade Sauce*
*16 large shrimp or prawn, steamed,*
  *chilled, drained and peeled tail shells*
  *left on*

Rémoulade Sauce: Set aside half the green onions and parsley. Place the rest in food processor or blender with pimento, mustard, vinegar, and horseradish. Blend to a paste, then stir into mayonnaise along with the reserved greens and remaining ingredients. Let stand 1 hour before serving, to let the flavors develop.

Prepare 4 small salad plates with the outer lettuce leaves. Place a small leaf in the center of each to serve as a cup and fill with the sauce. Surround with chilled shrimp. Serves 4.

# Teppan Yaki with Shrimp, Chicken and Meat

-Japanese-

1 whole chicken breast
  skinned and boned
2 tablespoons soy sauce
2 tablespoons sake
1 teaspoon unseasoned
  rice vinegar
1/4 pound tender boneless beef
  (Sirloin or tenderloin)
1/2 pound medium or large
  shrimp, peeled, deveined
Cooked rice
1 lemon cut into wedges
Sweet onion, sliced

Green onions, cut in 1-inch lengths
Red and green bell pepper, sliced
  crosswise and seeded
Fresh asparagus spears, cut diagonally
  into 2-inch lengths
1 small jewel or Garnet yam, sliced
1/8 inch thick
Large mushrooms, sliced 1/8 inch thick
Carrots, in thin diagonal slices
1 large daikon (Japanese giant radish)
A small pitcher of cooking oil
Soy sauce for dipping

Teppan Yaki is a cooking method rather than a particular dish. It is the kind of table top or tableside cooking practiced at some Japanese restaurants, usually with a lot of fan-fare and flashing knives.

Separate two muscles of the chicken breast halves. Cut smaller muscles lengthwise into 1/2x2-inch strips; cut larger muscles crosswise into strips 1/4 inch thick. Combine in small bowl with soy sauce, sake, and vinegar and marinate 30 minutes.

Slice beef thinly across grain (partially freezing meat, or partially thawing frozen meat, makes easier to slice thinly). Arrange beef slices and shrimp attractively on platter with bowl of chicken in center. Arrange sliced vegetables on second platter. Grate daikon on medium or fine side of a box grater.

Set each place with chopsticks, small bowl containing about 1/2 cup of grated daikon with its liquid, and another small bowl of rice. Place electric skillet on the table within reach of all the diners; heat to medium low and add enough oil to coat the bottom.

Have everyone join in cooking, placing raw food in skillet, turning them, and retrieving them when done, fondue style. While the first round is cooking, each diner can season his daikon to taste with soy sauce and lemon juice. (About 1 teaspoon soy and 1/8 of a lemon). Dip cooked foods in daikon mixture, then transfer them to your rice bowl to drain for few seconds. Continue adding food as space is available in skillet. Regulate heat so food cooks quickly but does not scorch and add more oil as needed. Eat the rice as you go along or save it for the end, when it has soaked up flavor from all the different ingredients. Serves 4.

## Shrimp Scampi with Vegetable Strips

*-Mediterranean-*
*1 tablespoon olive oil*
*1-1/2 pounds large or jumbo*
  *shrimp peeled and deveined*
  *with tail shells left on*
*2 large garlic cloves, minced*
*1 tablespoon minced shallots*
*2 tablespoons brandy*

*2 teaspoons lemon juice*
*1-1/2 tablespoons chopped Italian parsley*
*1/8 teaspoon salt*
*1/4 teaspoon freshly ground black pepper*
*4 tablespoons unsalted butter*

In large skillet, heat 1 tablespoon of the oil to near smoking. You can use more olive oil, if necessary. Add the shrimp and cook until just opaque in center; remove to warm plate.

Add a little more oil to pan if necessary and add garlic and shallots. Cook just until fragrant but not browned, about 10 seconds, then add brandy, lemon juice, parsley, salt, and pepper. Cook until well reduced, then remove pan from heat and swirl in butter.

Return shrimp to pan and toss them to coat with sauce. Arrange on individual plates, tails pointing outward. Spoon sauce over. Serves 4.

## Shrimp Broiled in Butter

*6 tablespoons unsalted butter*
*1 tablespoon whole fennel seeds*
*1/4 teaspoon freshly ground*
  *black pepper*

*2 tablespoons lemon juice*
*1 pound large shrimp, deveined*
  *through the shell*
*Rice pilaf (page 111)*

In heavy skillet, over medium heat, melt butter. Add fennel, pepper, salt and lemon juice and simmer 5 minutes. Remove from heat and set aside 15 to 30 minutes for flavors to mix.

Reheat skillet over medium-high heat until butter is quite bubbly. Add shrimp and cook, turning once, until shells turn pink. Place pan under the broiler and cook 4 to 5 minutes. Transfer shrimp to shallow serving dish or individual dishes and pour sauce over all. Peel shrimp and dip them in sauce, allowing some of fennel seeds to cling to shrimp. Spoon sauce over rice. Serves 4.

## Louisiana-Style Shrimp Creole

1 pound ripe tomatoes
3/4 teaspoon salt
1 teaspoon paprika
1/4 teaspoon each black and
  white pepper
1/8 teaspoon cayenne pepper
2 tablespoons unsalted butter or
  olive oil or a combination
1-1/2 pounds shrimp peeled
  and deveined
Hot pepper sauce to taste (optional)

1 cup finely diced onion
1/2 cup finely diced celery
2 cloves garlic, minced
1 large green or red bell pepper,
  finely diced
Small herb bouquet of thyme, or
  a combination marjoram, parsley
  bay leaf (tied with string or
  in cheesecloth)

Peel tomatoes, cut them in half, and squeeze out seeds into strainer, catching juice in small bowl. Discard seeds and chop tomatoes. Combine salt, paprika, and peppers in small bowl and set aside. Heat butter in large saucepan and sauté onion, celery, garlic, and bell pepper over medium heat until they soften. Add spice mixture and cook another minute, then add tomatoes with their juice and the herb bouquet. Simmer until mixture is slightly reduced, about 10 minutes. Remove herb bouquet. (The sauce may be made to this point a day ahead and refrigerated).

Return sauce to heat if made ahead. Taste for seasoning and adjust if needed. Add the shrimp and cook at a simmer until shrimp are opaque, 3 to 6 minutes depending on size. Serve with rice. Pass hot pepper sauce for seasoning at table, if desired. Serves 4.


## Grilled Shrimp from Cancun

-Mexican-
Marinade:
1/4 cup lemon or lime juice
2 tablespoons grenadine syrup
2 ounces tequila
3/4 teaspoon salt
1/4 teaspoon Tabasco

1 pound medium or large shrimp
  deveined in shell
Lime wedges

Combine the marinade ingredients in bowl; add shrimp, and marinate 30 minutes to 1 hour, turning occasionally. Do not marinate any longer or the lemon juice will cook the shrimp.

Drain shrimp and skewer them. Grill over a medium to hot fire or broil 3 inches from the heat until shells turn pink and the meat is opaque, 2 to 4 minutes per side. Serve with lime wedges. Serve these shrimp with chilled beer or margaritas. Serves 4.

## New England Clam Chowder

3 to 4 bacon slices, diced
1 onion, finely chopped
1/2 cup finely diced celery
2 tablespoons all-purpose flour
2 (6-1/2-oz.) cans chopped or
   minced clams, undrained
2 (8-oz.) bottles clam juice

3 medium potatoes, peeled,
   cut in 1/2-inch cubes
1 bay leaf
2-1/2 cups half and half
Salt, pepper, paprika
Parsley, finely chopped

In large kettle, fry bacon until crisp; drain on paper towels. Reserve 1 to 2 tablespoons bacon fat in kettle. Add onion and celery; sauté until onion is soft and transparent. Stir in flour; cook 1 minute. Drain juice from clams into kettle; reserve clams. Stir in bottled clam juice. Add cooked bacon, potatoes and bay leaf. Cover and simmer 20 minutes or until potatoes are tender. Add half and half and reserved clams. Add salt and pepper to taste. Cook until heated through. Remove and discard bay leaf. Serve from kettle or spoon into tureen. Garnish with paprika and parsley. Serves 4.

## Fisherman Wharf's Clam Chowder from San Francisco

1 medium onion, chopped
3/4 cup diced celery
1 garlic clove, minced
3/4 teaspoon finely chopped
   thyme or 1/4 teaspoon
   dried leaf thyme
1/2 teaspoon chopped sage or 1/8
   to 1/4 teaspoon dried leaf sage
2 tablespoons all-purpose flour
3 medium potatoes, peeled,
   cut in 3/4-inch cubes

2 (8-oz.) clam juice plus 2 cups water
1-1/2 lb firm texture skinless fish fillets
2 cups half and half
Salt
Freshly ground black pepper
1/8 teaspoon cayenne red pepper
Parsley, chopped
2 cups toasted croutons or oyster crackers

In large kettle, over medium-high heat, sauté onion until soft and transparent. Add celery, garlic, bay leaf, thyme, and sage. Stirring frequently, cook 2 to 3 minutes; stir in flour; stirring constantly, cook 1 to 2 minutes longer. Stir in potatoes and clam juice and water. Cover and simmer until potatoes are tender, 20 to 25 minutes. Cut fillets into 1-inch pieces; add to stock mixture. Simmer 5 minutes or until fish turns opaque and becomes firm. Remove and discard bay leaf. Stir in half and half; heat through. Add salt, black pepper and red pepper to taste. Spoon into tureen or serve in individual bowls. Garnish with parsley. Serve croutons or oyster crackers separately. Serves 6.

# Bouillabaisse

*-French-*

Soup croutons
Rouille
1/4 cup olive oil
2 medium onions, chopped
2 medium leeks, white and pale
   green portions only, chopped
4 garlic cloves, minced
4 cups fish stock
1 cup dry white wine
4 medium tomatoes, peeled, chopped
1/2 teaspoon fennel seeds, crushed
1/4 cup chopped parsley

1-1/2 teaspoons finely chopped thyme
1/2 to 3/4 teaspoon dried leaf thyme
1 bay leaf
1 teaspoon saffron threads or 1/8
   teaspoon powdered saffron
Salt
Freshly ground pepper
2 pound firm texture, skinless fish fillets
1 to 1-1/2 pound cooked, in-shell lobster
   tails, thawed if frozen
18 mussels, debearded
18 scallops

**Rouille:**

1 large, red bell pepper or
   2 (2-oz.) jars sliced pimentos,
   drained
1/2 cup soft white bread crumbs
1/4 cup milk or water

1/4 to1/2 teaspoon hot-pepper flakes
2 or 3 garlic cloves
1/4 cup olive oil
1 to 3 tablespoons broth from
   Bouillabaisse

Rouille: Roast bell pepper over an open flame or in broiler until skin is charred and blistered. Place in large plastic-food storage bag; set aside 5 to 10 minutes to steam. Peel blistered pepper; cut in half. Remove and discard seeds. In medium bowl, combine bread crumbs and milk or water; let stand 5 minutes. Squeeze crumbs dry; discard liquid. In blender or food processor fitted with metal blade, process bell-pepper strips or pimentos, hot pepper flakes, garlic and soaked bread crumbs until smooth. Gradually add oil until thoroughly blended. At serving time, stir in broth. Add salt to taste. Spoon into small serving bowl. Serve separately. Rouille can be spooned onto croutons to float in soup or spooned directly into Bouillabaisse. Makes 3/4 cup.

In large heavy kettle, over medium-high heat, heat oil. Add onions, leeks and garlic; over medium heat, sauté about 5 minutes. Add stock, wine, tomatoes, fennel seeds, parsley, thyme, bay leaf and saffron. Bring to boil; reduce heat and simmer 10 minutes. Season with salt and pepper to taste. Cut fish into pieces, about 2x1-1/2. Add fish pieces to stock mixture; gently simmer 2 to 3 minutes. With heavy knife or kitchen shears, cut lobster tails into 1-1/2-inch pieces, cutting through flesh and shell. Scrub mussels with a brush to remove dirt from shells; discard any mussels that do not close. Add lobster pieces and cleaned mussels to stock mixture. Cook until mussels open, 3 to 6 minutes; discard any mussels that do not open. During final 2 minutes of cooking, add scallops. Finish preparing Rouille. Remove and discard bay leaf. Serve soup from kettle or spoon into tureen. Place 1 or 2 croutons in individual bowls; ladle broth over croutons. Arrange fish and shellfish on top. Serve Rouille and remaining croutons separately. Serves 8.

# Maryland Blue Crab

1/4 cup seafood seasoning
2 tablespoons salt
2 cups white vinegar

2 cups beer or water
24 live blue crab or other crab
Beer

In large bowl, combine seafood seasoning, salt, vinegar and 2 cups beer or water; blend well.

Place 12 crabs in large steamer or pot with a raised rack and tight-fitting lid. Pour one-half of the seasoning liquid over crab. Add remaining crab. Pour remaining liquid over them. Cover and bring liquid to boil. Steam about 20 minutes; crab will turn bright red. To serve, cover table with thick layer of paper tablecloth. Provide wooden mallets, a paring knife and paper towels. Heap steamed crab in center of table. Serve with beer. Serves 12.

# Crab Imperial

1/4 cup butter or margarine
1 small onion, finely chopped
2 tablespoons all-purpose flour
1/8 teaspoon cayenne pepper
1/2 cup milk
1/2 cup half and half
2 tablespoons dry sherry
1/4 cup mayonnaise

2 teaspoons lemon juice
Salt
1 lb crab meat
3 to 4 tablespoons freshly grated
   parmesan cheese
1/4 to 1/2 teaspoon paprika, if desired
6 to 8 lemon wedges

Preheat oven to 450 °F. Butter 1-quart casserole or 6 to 8 small au gratin dishes set aside. In medium saucepan, melt 2 tablespoons butter or margarine. Add onion; sauté about 5 minutes. Blend in flour, red pepper and nutmeg. Cook 1 to 2 minutes, stirring constantly. Stir in milk, half and half and 2 tablespoons sherry. Cook until thick and smooth, 3 to 4 minutes. Stir in mayonnaise, 2 teaspoons lemon juice and salt. Taste and add more sherry, lemon juice and salt, if desired. Set aside. In large skillet, melt remaining 2 tablespoons butter or margarine. Flake crabmeat; remove any cartilage. Add flaked crabmeat to skillet. Stirring occasionally, cook over low heat 1 minute or until heated through. Gently fold in sauce. Spoon mixture into buttered casserole or small dishes. Sprinkle top with parmesan cheese and paprika, if desired. Bake 12 to 15 minutes or until mixture is lightly browned and bubbling. Serve with lemon wedges. Serves 6.

## Crab Las Brisas

Oil for deep frying
4 (9-inch) flour tortillas
3 tablespoons mayonnaise
3 tablespoons dairy sour cream
2 teaspoons mild green taco
  sauce or to taste
1/2 lb fresh crab meat, drained or
  1 (6-oz.) can cooked crab meat
3 cups shredded lettuce

3 green onions, sliced
1 tomato, diced
1 avocado, diced
1/3 cup sliced ripe olives
1/2 cup shredded Monterey jack or
  cheddar cheese
Dairy sour cream
Mild green taco sauce (optional)

Pour oil 2 to 3 inches deep into heavy saucepan. Heat to 370 °F or until a 1-inch cube of bread turns golden brown in 50 seconds. Holding a ladle in center of tortilla to form a cup, fry 1 tortilla in hot oil until crisp and golden brown. Drain on paper towels; repeat with remaining tortillas. In small bowl, combine mayonnaise, sour cream and 2 to 3 teaspoons taco sauce or to taste. If you are using fresh crab, prepare it as in Maryland Blue crab (page 106). Flake crabmeat into separate bowl; remove any cartilage. Add shredded lettuce and green onions. Toss mayonnaise mixture with crab mixture. Spoon crab mixture into center of tortilla cups. Top each with a sprinkling of tomato, avocado, olives and cheese. Spoon a dollop of sour cream on top of each. Serve with additional taco sauce, if desired. Serves 4.

## Crab Cakes

1 egg, slightly beaten
1 cup fresh bread crumbs
1/4 cup mayonnaise
1/4 cup finely chopped parsley
1 teaspoon Worcestershire sauce
1/2 to 1 teaspoon seafood
  seasoning or crab seasoning

1/4 teaspoon dry mustard
1/8 teaspoon cayenne pepper
Salt and black pepper
1 pound crabmeat
2 tablespoons butter or margarine
2 tablespoons vegetable oil

In medium bowl, combine egg, 3/4 cup bread crumbs, mayonnaise, parsley, Worcestershire sauce, seafood seasoning or crab seasoning, mustard and red pepper. Add salt and black pepper to taste. Gentle fold in crabmeat. Shape mixture into 6 balls; flatten each into 3-inch cakes. Coat crab cakes with remaining 1/4 cup bread crumbs; place coated crab cakes on platter. Cover; refrigerate 1 hour.

In large skillet, heat 1 tablespoon butter or margarine and 1 tablespoon oil. Pan-fry crab cakes 3 to 4 minutes on each side or until golden brown. Add more butter or margarine and oil to skillet as necessary. Serve with lemon wedges. Serves 6.

# Pan-Fried Oysters with Seafood Sauce

Seafood Cocktail sauce:
1/2 cup tomato-based chili sauce
1 tablespoon horseradish
1 tablespoon lemon juice
2 teaspoons Worcestershire sauce
1/4 teaspoon salt
1/8 teaspoon cayenne pepper

Seafood Cocktail Sauce
40 oysters, shucked
Vegetable oil for deep frying
Lemon wedges
Salt
Freshly ground pepper
3/4 cup yellow corn meal

Seafood Cocktail Sauce: In small bowl, combine all ingredients. Cover and refrigerate at least 2 hours to let flavors blend.

Drain oysters; pat dry with paper towels. If oysters are large, cut in half. Set aside. Preheat oven 165 °F. In heavy saucepan, heat oil to 365 °F or until a 1-inch cube of bread turns golden brown in 1 minute. Season oysters with salt and pepper. Pour cornmeal into a shallow bowl. Roll seasoned oysters in cornmeal, coating completely. Fry 4 or 5 coated oysters at a time until coating is crisp and golden brown. Do not overcook. Drain on paper towels. Keep warm in oven until all are cooked. Serve with seafood cocktail sauce and lemon wedges. Serves 6-8.

# Scallop Marsala

1-1/2 pound scallops
3 tablespoons butter or margarine
2 tablespoons shallots,
  finely chopped or white portions
  of green onions
1/2 pound small mushrooms,
  sliced

3/4 cup whipping cream
4 tablespoons Marsala or Madeira wine
Salt
White pepper
Chervil or parsley, finely chopped

Cut large scallops in half horizontally. In large skillet, melt half of butter or margarine. Add shallots or green onions and mushrooms, over medium-high heat sauté about 3 minutes. Spoon into medium bowl and set aside. In skillet, melt remaining butter or margarine. Add scallops, sauté 1 to 2 minutes or until scallops are opaque. Do not overcook. Use slotted spoon to add scallops to mushroom mixture; set aside. Add cream and wine to liquid in skillet; add liquid from cooked scallops and mushrooms. Cook over medium-high heat until sauce reduces to 2/3 to 3/4 cup and thickens enough to coat a spoon lightly. Add reserved mushroom mixture and scallops and heat through. Season with salt and white pepper to taste. Serves 6.

# RICE PILAF

# Rice Pilaf-Sade Pilav

*-Turkish-*

4 cups water
2 cups regular long
   grain rice

1-1/2 tablespoon butter or margarine
1/4 teaspoon salt

In large saucepan with tight-fitting lid, over high heat, heat water to boiling. Add rice, salt and butter or margarine. Reduce heat until mixture just simmers; with fork stir once and cover pan, simmer without stirring or lifting lid, until rice is tender and all liquid is absorbed. Check tenderness by tasting a grain. Remove from heat, cover with clean kitchen towel, place the lid over the towel. The towel will absorb the excess of water steam. Serves 4-6.

# Rice Pilaf with Tomatoes-Domatesli Pilav

*-Turkish-*

4 cups water
2 cups regular long grain rice
1 large tomatoes, finely chopped

2 tablespoons butter or margarine
1-1/2 teaspoon mixed spices
Salt to taste

In large saucepan with tight-fitting lid, over high heat, heat water to boiling, add rice, salt, mixed spices and butter. Just before reducing the heat add chopped tomatoes, stir once or twice. And cover pan and simmer without stirring or lifting lid until rice is tender and all liquid is absorbed. Check tenderness by tasting a grain. Remove from heat, cover with clean kitchen towel and place the lid over the towel. Let stand 20-25 minutes for drier rice pilaf. Serves 4.

# Rice Pilaf with Vegetables

*-Turkish-*

4 cups water
2 cups regular long grain rice
2 tablespoons butter or
   margarine

1 carrot, sliced thinly
1/2 cup frozen peas, thawed and drained
Salt to taste
1 tablespoon minced fresh dill

In large saucepan with tight-fitting lid, over high heat, heat water to boiling. Add rice, salt, dill weed, peas and sliced carrots. Reduce heat until mixture just simmers; with fork, stir once or twice. Cover pan and simmer without stirring or lifting lid until rice is tender and all liquid is absorbed. Check tenderness by tasting grain. Serve with chicken and meat meals. Serves 4.

## Rice Pilaf with Raisins and Almonds-Üzümlü ve Bademli Pilav

-Turkish-

4 cups water
2 cups beef broth
3 cups regular long
  grain rice
3 tablespoons butter or
  margarine

3/4 cup dried seedless raisins
1/4 cup blanched almond
  slices (optional)
Salt to taste
1 teaspoon cinnamon
1/8 teaspoon black pepper

In small saucepan, over medium heat, in 1/2 tablespoon melted butter or margarine, lightly roast almonds, about 10 minutes. Remove from heat and place into small cup; and set aside.

In large saucepan with tight-fitting lid, over high heat, heat water to boiling, add beef broth, rice, salt and rest of the butter or margarine.

Reduce heat until mixture just simmers, add cinnamon and pepper; with fork stir once or twice. Cover pan and simmer without stirring or lifting lid until rice is tender and all liquid is absorbed. Check tenderness by tasting a grain. Add raisins 5 to 7 minutes before removing the pilaf from heat. Before serving add toasted almonds and stir once or twice. Serves 6.

## Ottoman-Style Pilaf

-Turkish-

3 cups water
2 cups regular long grain rice
1/2 pound lamb meat, cut
  1/2-inch thick small cubes
Water for lamb meat
3/4 cup finely chopped
  Mediterranean parsley
1/2 cup thinly sliced red onion

2 tablespoons margarine
1 medium carrot, chopped
1/4 cup blanched whole almonds
Black pepper
Salt
Sliced red onion (optional)

In medium saucepan, over high heat, heat water and lamb meat. Cook for 2 hours. When lamb meat is done add salt to taste. Reserve remaining liquid.

In large saucepan with tight-fitting lid, over medium heat, heat margarine, add whole almonds, cook for 2 minutes. Add 3 cups water and 1 cup of reserved lamb liquid; heat to boiling; add rice, chopped carrots, pepper and cooked lamb meat. Cover pan and simmer without stirring or lifting lid, about 15 minutes or until rice is tender and all liquid is absorbed. Garnish with sliced red onion and chopped Turkish/Italian parsley. Serves 4-6.

## Anatolian-Style Rice Pilaf

*-Turkish-*

*2 cups long grain rain rice*
*2 cups hot chicken broth*
*2 cups hot water*
*1 medium chicken breast, cut*
  *into 1/2-inch thick pieces*
*3/4 cup beef or chicken heart*
  *pieces or lamb meat cubes*
*1 tablespoon sugar*

*1 medium carrot cut into small cubes*
*3 tablespoons margarine*
*1 medium onion*
*1 tablespoon pinenuts*
*2 tablespoons currants*
*1 tablespoon minced fresh dill*
*Salt*
*1/2 teaspoon allspice*
*1/2 teaspoon cinnamon*

In medium saucepan, over medium heat, sauté chicken and heart pieces. Remove from heat; set aside.

In large saucepan with tight-fitting lid, over medium heat, in 2 tablespoons margarine, sauté chopped onion. Add pinenuts cook until nuts change their colors. Add rice, stir a few times. Then add hot chicken broth and water. And add salt, allspice, cinnamon, sugar, currants and minced dill. Cover pan and simmer until rice is tender. After rice is done add sautéed chicken and heart pieces, stir once or twice.

If you like, thoroughly grease a 5-1/2-inch cup ring mold. Lightly pack the rice mixture in ring mold; let stand 1 minute. Loosen edges; invert plate on top of mold; holding mold and plate, quickly invert rice ring onto plate. Lift of mold. Serves 4-6.

# POTATOES

## Pan-Roasted Potatoes

6 medium potatoes, peeled
1 teaspoon salt
Water

Paprika, parsley or thyme
leaves

In 3-quart saucepan over high heat, heat potatoes, salt and water to cover potatoes to boiling. Reduce heat to low; cover and simmer 10 minutes. Drain potatoes; arrange around beef, chicken or turkey in roasting pan; turn to coat with drippings in pan. Bake 40 to 60 minutes at 325 °F along with roast, turning occasionally, just until tender and evenly browned all over. Before serving sprinkle potatoes with paprika, parsley or thyme. If you are serving with roast; arrange around roast on platter. Serves 6.

## Potatoes au Gratin

3 tablespoons butter or margarine
6 medium potatoes, peeled and
    thinly sliced
1-1/2 teaspoons salt

1 cup shredded cheddar cheese
1/2cup fresh bread crumbs

Preheat oven to 425 °F. In 12x8-inch baking pan, in oven, melt butter. Remove from oven. Add potatoes and salt; toss together and arrange potatoes in even layer in baking pan. Sprinkle layers with cheese and top with remaining cheese and bread crumbs. Cover with foil. Bake 20 minutes; uncover and bake 15 minutes more or until potatoes are tender. Serves 6.

## Herbed Potato Casseroles

8 medium potatoes
3 teaspoons mixed spices
2-1/2 cups shredded Swiss
    cheese

1 tablespoon minced parsley
Salt and pepper to taste
1 to 2 tablespoons margarine
2 teaspoons onion powder
1/2 teaspoon garlic powder

In large kettle, boil potatoes until they are soft enough to mash. Peel and mash them into large bowl. Add remaining ingredients and 2 cups shredded Swiss cheese. Mix well. Spoon the mixture into 6 small casseroles. Sprinkle tops with 1/2 cup shredded cheese. Bake them in 375 °F oven until tops turn golden. Serve with meat, chicken or turkey dishes. Serves 6.

## Pommes Anna

*2 tablespoons butter or*
*margarine*
*1 teaspoon salt*
*1 teaspoon lemon-pepper*
*seasoning*

*2 teaspoons parsley*
*3 large potatoes, peeled*

In 1-quart saucepan over low heat, melt butter with salt. Preheat oven to 425 °F. Slice potatoes about 1/4-inch thick. In greased 8-inch pie plate, arrange potato slices, overlapping them; drizzle butter mixture on top. Cover plate tightly with foil; bake 20 minutes. Uncover and bake about 55 minutes more or until potatoes are very tender and crusty. Let stand at room temperature 5 minutes. With metal spatula, carefully loosen potatoes from pie plate. Place inverted plate over potatoes; holding both plates, invert and unmold. Cut into wedges. Serves 6.

## Potato and Vegetable Pie

*3 cups shredded potato*
*1 egg, beaten*
*1/4 cup grated parmesan*
*cheese*
*1-1/2 cups thinly sliced*
*yellow squash and zucchini*
*1 small sweet red pepper,*
*coarsely chopped*
*1 tablespoon butter or*
*margarine*

*1/2 tablespoon snapped fresh*
*basil or 1/2 teaspoon*
*dried basil*
*1/2 cup diced cooked ham*
*1/4 cup milk*
*2 eggs, beaten*
*3 ounces Monterey jack cheese,*
*shredded*

Mix together 3 cups shredded potato, 1 egg and parmesan cheese. Press into bottom and up sides of greased 9-inch pie plate or quiche dish. Bake in a 400°F oven for 15 minutes. Meanwhile, in large skillet, over medium heat, in butter cook squash, zucchini and sweet red pepper about 5 minutes, stirring occasionally. Remove from heat. Cool 1 minute. Stir in basil, 1/4 teaspoon salt, 1/8 teaspoon pepper, and ham. Combine milk and the 2 eggs; add to skillet along with jack cheese. Pour the mixture into pie plate. Bake, uncovered, 15 minutes or until set. Let stand 5 minutes before serving. Serves 8.

# PASTAS

## Manicotti

*-Italian-*

| | |
|---|---|
| 1 package Manicotti | 1 tablespoon chopped parsley |
| 1 (15 oz.) ricotta cheese | 1/4 teaspoon salt |
| 2 cups shredded mozzarella cheese | 1/4 teaspoon pepper |
| 1/2 cup grated parmesan cheese | 1/4 teaspoon basil |
| 1 egg(optional) | 1/8 teaspoon nutmeg |

*Turkish version of Tomato-Basil sauce:*

| | |
|---|---|
| 3 large tomatoes, peeled and diced | 1 tablespoon tomato paste |
| 3/4 teaspoon basil | 1/4 teaspoon salt |
| 1 garlic clove, minced | 1/2 teaspoon sugar |
| 1/2 small onion, minced | 1 tablespoon minced parsley |
| Water | 1 teaspoon all purpose flour |

Tomato-Basil Sauce: In small cup, over medium heat, melt butter or margarine, add 1-1/2 cup water and rest of the ingredients, cook, stirring until sauce thickens. Serve hot over manicotti.

Prepare pasta as directed on package; drain. Rinse with cold water, drain and arrange in single layer to fill. Meanwhile, mix ricotta cheese, 1-1/2 cups of mozzarella cheese, 1/4 cup parmesan cheese, 1 egg (optional), parsley, salt, pepper, basil and nutmeg. Spoon mixture into manicotti shells, using at least 1/3 cup per shell. Place filled manicotti shells in a single layer in greased medium baking pan. Pour Tomato-Basil sauce over manicotti shells. Sprinkle with remaining 1/2 cup mozzarella cheese and 1/4 cup parmesan cheese; bake at 375 °F until cheese is melted. Serves 4-6.

## Pasta with Vegetable Strips

*-Italian-*

| | |
|---|---|
| 1 Package Farfelle pasta | 1 zucchini, cut in strips |
| 2 tablespoons olive oil | 2 medium carrots, cut in strips |
| 3 tablespoons butter | 1 cup fresh green beans, cut in strips |
| Salt | 1/2 cup green and red peppers, cut in strips |
| Parsley | Parmesan cheese |
| Cayenne pepper | |

Prepare pasta as label directs. Drain well and return to the saucepan, add 1 tablespoon olive oil; mix it; keep it warm. Meanwhile in small saucepan, heat butter, add salt, parsley, pepper and vegetable strips; cook until vegetables are crisp-tender. Combine hot vegetable strips with pasta. Serve with parmesan cheese. Serves 4.

## Stuffed Shells

*-Italian-*

1 (16-oz.) package jumbo
   shells
3 cups ricotta cheese or 1 cup ricotta
   and 2 cups Turkish white cheese
1 (8-oz.) package mozzarella
   cheese, shredded
1/2 cup grated parmesan cheese
Tomato-Basil Sauce (page 121)

1 egg
1 teaspoon mixed spices
1/4 cup chopped parsley
1 teaspoon salt
1/4 teaspoon cayenne pepper
1/4 teaspoon dried mint

Prepare shells as label directs; drain well in colander. Preheat oven to 350 °F. In large bowl, combine ricotta, Turkish white (feta), mozzarella, parmesan cheeses, egg, mixed spices, parsley, salt, pepper and mint.

Stuff rounded tablespoon of cheese mixture into each shell and place them into 13x9-inch baking dishes. Spoon the sauce over the shells and sprinkle with parmesan cheese. Bake 30 minutes. Serves 8-10.


## Rigatoni and Meat Balls

*-Italian-*

7-oz. prepared rigatoni
Sauce:
4 medium tomatoes, seeded
   and chopped
1 cup sliced fresh mushrooms
1 can (6-oz.) tomato paste
1/4 cup water
1 teaspoon Italian seasoning
1/2 teaspoon sugar
1/8 teaspoon pepper

Meatballs:
1 pound lean ground beef
1 egg white
2 tablespoons grated parmesan cheese
2 tablespoons seasoned dry bread crumbs
2 tablespoons skim milk
3/4 teaspoon Italian seasoning
1 tablespoon vegetable oil
1 cup shredded mozzarella cheese

In medium saucepan, over medium heat, combine sauce ingredients. Cook until mixture boils. Reduce heat to medium-low and cook, uncovered, for 20 minutes, stirring occasionally.

Thoroughly combine meatball ingredients. Shape into 18 meatballs. In large skillet, heat oil over medium heat. Add meatballs, cook until firm and brown on all sides, about 15 minutes. Drain. In 3-quart casserole arrange meatballs on cooked rigatoni and cover with sauce. Cover with aluminum foil. Bake at 350 °F for 15 minutes. Add cheese; bake for 10 minutes longer, until mixture bubbles. Serves 6.

# Cannelloni at San Marco

*-Italian-*

*Homemade pasta dough:*
*2-1/4 to 2-1/2 cups all purpose flour*
*1/3 cup water*
*2 eggs*
*1 egg yolk*
*1 tablespoon olive oil*
*1 teaspoon salt*

*Parmesan Cheese Sauce:*
*1/4 cup butter*
*1/4 cup all-purpose flour*
*1-1/2 cups half-and-half*
*1-1/2 cups water*
*2 chicken-flavor bouillon cubes*
*1/2 cup grated parmesan cheese*

*Filling:*
*1 tablespoon chopped green onion*
*1 (10-oz.) package frozen chopped*
*    spinach, cooked and drained*
*1 cup finely chopped cooked chicken*
*1/2 cup finely chopped cooked ham*
*1/2 cup grated parmesan cheese*
*1 egg, beaten*
*1 tablespoon dry sherry*
*1/4 teaspoon ground ginger*
*Salt*
*Salad oil*
*5 quarts water*
*Chopped parsley for garnish*
*2 tablespoons margarine*

Homemade pasta dough: In large bowl, combine 1 cup flour and remaining ingredients. With mixer at low speed, beat 2 minutes, occasionally scraping bowl. With wooden spoon, stir in enough additional flour to make a soft dough. Turn dough onto lightly floured surface, knead until smooth and elastic, about 10 minutes. Cover dough and let rest 30 minutes.

Cannelloni: Cut prepared dough into 3 pieces. On well-floured surface with floured rolling pin, roll 1 piece into 16x8-inch rectangle. With knife, cut the dough rectangle into eight 4-inch squares. Place squares on floured, clean cloth towel. Repeat with remaining dough, making 24 squares in all. Cover; let stand 30 minutes.

In 2-quart saucepan over medium heat, in butter, cook onion until tender. Stir in spinach, chicken, ham, parmesan cheese, egg, dry sherry, ground ginger and 1/4 teaspoon salt; set aside.

Preheat oven to 350 °F. Grease 13x9 inch baking dish. In 8-quart saucepot, heat to boiling water, 2 tablespoons salt and 1 tablespoon oil. Cook squares a few at a time, 5 minutes. Remove pasta with slotted spoon; drain in colander and assemble while warm.

To assemble cannelloni: with spoon, spread rounded tablespoon of meat mixture across center of warm pasta square. Roll jell-roll fashion. Place, seam side down, in pan. Repeat with remaining pasta squares and meat mixture. Prepare cheese sauce.

Parmesan Cheese Sauce: In 2-quart saucepan over medium heat, into hot butter, stir flour until well blended. Gradually stir in half-and-half, water and chicken bouillon cubes. Cook, stirring constantly, until sauce is thickened. Stir in the grated parmesan cheese and heat just until melted.

Pour cheese sauce over cannelloni; sprinkle with parsley. Bake in oven 20 minutes then broil 5 minutes. Serves 6-8.

# Eggplant Lasagna

-Italian-
Spaghetti sauce
1/2 (16-oz.) package lasagna
  noodles
3/4 cup dried bread crumbs
1/4 teaspoon pepper
Salt
1 egg

2 tablespoons water
1 medium eggplant, cut in1/2-inch slices
Salad oil
1 (16-oz.) package mozzarella cheese,
  thinly sliced
1/4 cup grated parmesan cheese

Cook lasagna noodles as label directs; drain. On waxed paper, combine crumbs, pepper and 1/2 teaspoon salt. In small dish with fork, beat egg with water. Dip eggplant into egg mixture, then crumb mixture.

In large skillet over medium heat, in 2 tablespoons hot salad oil, cook eggplant slices a few at a time, until tender, adding more oil when necessary. Drain on paper towels.

Preheat oven to 350 °F. In 13x9 inch baking pan layer half of noodles, eggplant slices, mozzarella and spaghetti sauce and repeat. Sprinkle with parmesan cheese. Bake 30 minutes or until hot. Serves 6-8.


# Baked Macaroni and Cheese

2 quarts water
Salt
1 (8-oz.) package elbow macaroni
4 tablespoons butter or margarine
3/4 cup fresh bread crumbs

1 small onion, minced
1 tablespoon all purpose flour
1/4 teaspoon dry mustard
1/8 teaspoon pepper
1-1/2 cups milk
2 cups shredded cheddar cheese

In large saucepan, heat to boiling, water and 1 teaspoon salt. Add macaroni; cook until tender but firm; drain. Grease 2-quart baking dish. Preheat oven to 350 °F.

In small saucepan, over medium heat, melt 2 tablespoons butter or margarine; add bread crumbs and toss to coat; set aside. Meanwhile, in 2-quart saucepan over medium heat, melt remaining butter; add onion and cook until tender, about 5 minutes.

Blend in flour, mustard, pepper and 1 teaspoon salt. Stir in milk; cook, stirring, until thickened. Remove from heat; stir in cheese.

Place macaroni in baking dish. Pour cheese mixture over macaroni. Sprinkle crumb mixture over top. Bake in oven 20 minutes. Serves to:4

## Spaghetti with Four Cheeses

*-Italian-*
*1 (8-oz.) package spaghetti*
*1/4 cup margarine*
*1 tablespoon all-purpose flour*
*1-1/2 cups half-and-half*
*1 cup shredded mozzarella*

*1 cup shredded fontina cheese*
*1/2 cup grated provolone cheese*
*1/4 cup grated parmesan or*
*    romano cheese*
*1/4 teaspoon salt*
*1/4 teaspoon cracked pepper*
*1 tablespoon chopped parsley*

Prepare spaghetti as label directs; drain well in colander and keep hot. Meanwhile, in large saucepan over medium heat, in hot margarine, stir in flour until blended; cook 30 seconds. Gradually stir in half-and-half; cook, stirring, until mixture boils and slightly thickens. Stir in mozzarella, fontina, provolone and parmesan cheeses, salt and pepper cooking until smooth and cheese is melted.

Pour hot spaghetti into warm, large bowl. Pour cheese sauce over spaghetti; sprinkle with parsley. Toss until spaghetti is well coated. Serves to: 4

## Chicken Penne with Artichokes

*-California style-*
*1 package penne*
*1 (10 oz.) package artichoke hearts*
*1 cup ripe olives, sliced*
*4 chicken breasts, cut into 1 to*
*    1-1/2 inch thick chunks*
*2 tablespoons lemon juice*

*Cheese sauce:*
*1/4 cup butter*
*1/4 tablespoon all-purpose flour*
*1-1/2 cups half and half*
*1 cup water*
*1/2 cup white wine*
*2 chicken-flavor bouillon cubes*
*2 cups grated parmesan and*
*    fontina cheese*
*Cracked black pepper to taste*
*Salt to taste*

Prepare penne as label directs; drain well and set aside, keep warm. In medium saucepan heat water, lemon juice and the artichoke hearts; cook until tender. Remove from the heat, drain well. In large skillet, in hot margarine cook chicken pieces until they are tender. In large pan, combine macaroni, chicken, artichoke and sliced ripe olives. Keep warm.

Cheese Sauce: In medium saucepan, over medium heat, in hot butter, stir in flour until well blended. Gradually stir in half and half, water, white wine, cracked black pepper, salt and chicken bouillon cubes. Cook, stirring constantly, until sauce is lightly thickened. Stir in the grated parmesan and fontina cheese and heat just until melted.

Pour hot cheese sauce over the chicken-artichoke mixture, toss it gently. Before serving, warm it in 350 °F oven until hot. Serves 4.

# Chicken Pepper Pasta

*-California style-*
6 tablespoons margarine
1 medium onion, cut in thin
  wedges
1 medium red bell pepper,
  cut in strips
1 medium yellow bell pepper,
  cut in strips
1 teaspoon minced garlic
3 skinless, boneless chicken
  breast halves cut into
  3x1/2-inch strips

1 tablespoon finely chopped
  fresh tarragon
3/4 teaspoon salt
1/4 teaspoon cracked black pepper
1 (7-ounce) package Creamette
  vermicelli uncooked
3/4 cup half and half
1 cup shredded mozzarella cheese
1/2 cup grated parmesan cheese

In large skillet, melt margarine until sizzling. Stir in onion, peppers and garlic. Cook over medium-high heat until peppers are crispy tender (2 to 3 minutes). Remove vegetables from skillet with slotted spoon, set aside, reserving juices in pan. Add chicken, tarragon, salt and pepper. Continue cooking, stirring occasionally, until chicken is lightly browned and fork tender (7 to 9 minutes). Prepare Creamette vermicelli according to package directions; drain. Add vegetables, half and half, mozzarella and parmesan cheese to chicken mixture; reduce heat to medium and continue cooking until cheese is melted (3 to 5 minutes). Add vermicelli, toss gently to coat. Serve immediately. Serves 6.

# PASTRIES and BREADS

## Turkish Pastry "Böreks" Baked in a Tray

The Turkish region of Thrace is famous for its böreks (1/2 to 2-inch thick, baked layers of filling and Yufka or phyllo sheets). Because the cheese, yogurt and milk are of very high quality, böreks are extremely rich and delicious. They are made of spinach, ground beef, herbs, cheese, eggs, margarine, milk and yogurt. Thracian böreks also have intricate toppings in which the phyllo is twisted to resemble ribbons, bow ties and even flattened carnations. Water böreks, baked in a tray, is another kind. This superb creation is a jewel in the crown of the börek family and is the final and perfect outcome of the process that began when Turks rolled the first dough in their Central Asian homeland almost a millennium ago. Other types of Turkish böreks include puf börek (puffy pastry dough stuffed and fried), bohça (yogurt based pastry stuffed and baked), sigara (cigarette shaped stuffed and fried pastry), muska (triangular shaped stuffed pastry) and tepsi (yufka-phyllo pie baked in a tray).

Turkish pastry called "Yufka" are the sheets of pastry rolled out very thinly, and correspond to the phyllo pastry in Greek cuisine. Yufka is more moist and thicker than phyllo. Making yufka is an extremely time-consuming process and for this reason the job is often left to the yufkaci (yufka-maker). The sheets of pastry can also be bought ready-made in Turkish shops.

## Spinach Filled Phyllo-Ispanakli Muska Böregi

*-Turkish-*
*2 tablespoons olive oil*
*1 medium onion, diced*
*1 (10-ounce) package frozen chopped spinach, thawed and squeezed dry*
*1 egg*

*1/3 cup shredded Turkish casserie or havarti cheese*
*1/4 teaspoon black pepper*
*1/3 pound Turkish pastry (yufka) or phyllo sheets*
*Salad oil for frying*
*1 tablespoon yogurt*

Before starting to cook, see (page 129). Since phyllo (fillo) dough is available in most markets, measurements in this recipe are written for phyllo dough. In 2-quart saucepan over medium heat, in hot oil, sauté onion until tender, stirring occasionally. Add spinach, salt and pepper, cook 6 to 7 minutes. Remove from heat; stir in cheese.

In small cup, mix the egg and yogurt. With knife, cut phyllo lengthwise into 2-inch wide strips. Place strips on waxed paper then cover slightly damp towel. Brush one strip of phyllo lightly with yogurt-egg mixture and place 1 teaspoonful spinach mixture at short end of strip. Fold one corner of strip diagonally over filling so the short edge meets the long edge, forming a right angle. Continue folding over at right angles until you reach the end of the strip to form a triangular-shape package (muska shape). To secure ends, dip ends into water filled bowl. This way ends stick on triangles. Repeat with remaining phyllo strips and spinach filling. In large frying pan over medium-high heat, in hot salad oil, fry böreks until golden on both sides. Remove to serving plate with slotted spoon. Serves 15.

## Herbed Ground Beef Filled Phyllo Baked In A Tray-Kiymali Börek

*-Turkish-*

| | |
|---|---|
| 1-1/4 pound ground beef | 3 tablespoons margarine, melted |
| 1 small green bell pepper, diced | 1-1/3 to 1-1/2 cups milk |
| 2 small tomatoes, peeled and diced | 2 tablespoons plain yogurt (optional) |
| 1/2 cup finely chopped parsley | 2 eggs |
| Black pepper and salt to taste | 1 (16 oz.) package Turkish pastry sheets (yufka) or phyllo sheets |

Before starting to cook take a look at (page 129). Since phyllo (fillo) dough is available in most markets, measurements in this recipe are written for phyllo dough. In large skillet, over medium heat, in 1 tablespoon hot margarine, sauté chopped onion until tender. Add ground beef, cook until pink color is gone. Add green bell pepper, tomatoes, parsley, salt and black pepper to taste; cook until half of the juice is evaporated. Remove from the heat. Pour 3 tablespoons melted margarine and milk in separate small bowls, mix yogurt (optional) and eggs in an another small bowl. Grease large pan, lay out one sheet of phyllo, brush with melted margarine, lay out another sheet of phyllo, brush with yogurt and egg mixture, lay out one more sheet of phyllo, brush with milk. After using about 8 sheets of phyllo, sprinkle on half of the ground beef mixture. Use another three sheets of phyllo, brushing each phyllo with milk and yogurt-egg mixture; sprinkle on rest of the ground beef mixture. Continue to make layers with rest of the phyllo and rest of the margarine, milk, yogurt-egg mixture. After using the last couple of phyllo, brush the top with egg and yogurt mixture. Let it rest for 25 to 30 minutes. (With this process layers of börek will absorb milk and you will have thicker and softer börek as in original Turkish börek with yufka. If you are using Turkish pastry sheets you will not need this process, you will just use less milk. And, you will be brushing layers just to moisten).

Bake börek at 350 °F for 45 minutes or until the top is golden. Remove from heat, let it cool, cut 3x3 squares and serve with fruit juices, tea or ayran (page 129) Serves 6.


## Herbed Ground Beef Topped-Thin Turkish Pizza-Kiymali Pide

*-Turkish-*

| | |
|---|---|
| 2 prepared frozen bread dough loaves, thawed | Salt and black pepper to taste |
| 1/2 pound ground beef | Parsley, finely chopped |
| 1 green bell pepper, diced | 2 teaspoons mixed spices |
| 1 medium onion, finely chopped | 2 medium tomatoes, peeled and diced |
| | Margarine |
| | Ayran to serve with pide |

You can prepare pide with variety of fillings such as spicy Turkish sausage (Sucuk)-

egg, and cheese-egg mixture. In large skillet, in 1 to 2 tablespoons margarine, sauté onion until tender. Add green pepper. Add ground beef, cook until pink color is gone, add tomatoes, parsley, salt and black pepper. Cook until most of the juice is evaporated. Set aside.

Thaw dough. Divide into 4 pieces; shape into oval balls, flatten dough pieces until 1/2-inch thick. Press dough to within 1/2-inch of edges, like preparing thin oval pizza crust. Spread cooked ground beef mixture on ovals. Bake them at 375 °F for 25-30 minutes or until top is golden. Brush edge of crusts with melted butter. Serve with Ayran. Ayran is a cold drink made with yogurt and water. Blend 5 to 6 tablespoons of yogurt with 1 to 2 tablespoons water. Pour into glasses; if you like sprinkle with salt and add ice cubes. Makes 1 glass of ayran. Instead of ground beef, you can use sucuk (Turkish sausage) and 6 eggs. Beat eggs, divide dough into 4 pieces, shape them as described above, top with sliced sucuk and beaten egg; bake at 375 °F for 30 minutes. Serves to 4.

## Pancakes

1-1/4 cups all-purpose flour
2 tablespoons sugar
2 teaspoons double-acting
 powder
3/4 teaspoon salt
1 egg
1-1/3 cups milk (for thicker
 pancakes, use only 1 cup milk)

Salad oil
Unsalted butter or margarine
Maple or maple-flavor syrup
Honey, preserves, marmalade,
 Turkish fruit preserves or
 apple butter as desired

In large bowl, mix first 4 ingredients. In small bowl, beat egg slightly; stir in milk and 3 tablespoons oil; add to flour mixture and stir just until flour is moistened. Heat skillet or griddle over medium-high heat until drop of water sizzles. Brush lightly with oil. Pour batter by scant 1/4 cupfuls onto hot skillet or griddle, making a few pancakes at a time. Cook until bubbly and bubbles burst; edges will look dry. With pancake turner, turn and cook until underside is golden. Place on heated platter; keep warm. Repeat, brushing skillet with more oil, if needed. Serve with butter, syrup, Turkish fruit preserves. Almost all of the Turkish fruit preserves such as Morello cherries, quince, apricot and strawberry have an extraordinary delicious and fresh taste.You can find them in Mediterranean, Middle Eastern, and Turkish food stores. Makes 12 pancakes.

# Waffles

1-3/4 cups all-purpose flour
1 teaspoon double-acting powder
1 teaspoon baking soda

1/2 teaspoon salt
2 cups buttermilk
1/3 cup salad oil
2 eggs

Preheat waffle baker as manufacturer directs. In large bowl whisk together flour, baking powder, baking soda and salt. Add buttermilk, salad oil and eggs to flour mixture and beat until thoroughly blended. Pour batter into center of lower half of baker until it spreads to about 1-inches from edges. Cover and bake as manufacturer directs; do not lift the cover during baking time. Loosen baked waffle carefully with fork. Preheat baker before pouring next waffle. Makes 5 waffles.

# Braid-Paskalya

3/4 to 1 cup sugar
1/2 teaspoon salt
1-1/2 packages active dry yeast
4 to 5 cups all purpose flour
1 cup milk
1/2 cup unsalted butter or
   margarine

1 egg
5 teaspoons mahlep
1 tablespoon all-purpose flour
1 egg yolk, slightly beaten
Whole almond pieces

You can find mahlep in Middle Eastern grocery stores. In large bowl, combine sugar, salt, yeast and 1 cup flour. In 2-quart saucepan over low heat, slowly heat milk and butter until very warm. With mixer at low speed, gradually beat liquid into dry ingredients. Increase speed to medium; beat 2 minutes more, occasionally scraping bowl with rubber spatula. Beat in egg and 1 cup flour; continue beating 2 minutes, occasionally scraping bowl. With spoon, stir in enough additional flour (about 2 cups) to make soft dough. Turn dough onto lightly floured surface; knead until smooth and elastic, about 10 minutes. Shape into a ball. Turn over in greased large bowl to grease top, cover; let it rise in warm place until dough is doubled, about 1 hour.

Punch down dough. On lightly floured surface, divide into 3 pieces. Roll each dough piece into a 12x4 strip. On greased cookie sheet, braid 3 rolls, tucking ends under. Cover; let rise until doubled, about 1 hour. Brush braid with beaten egg yolk. Top with whole almond pieces. Preheat oven to 350 °F. Bake 35 minutes or until golden and loaf sounds hollow when tapped. Remove to cool on wire rack. Makes 1 large braid.

# Dinner Rolls

1/3 cup sugar
1-1/2 teaspoons salt
2 packages active dry yeast
4-1/2 to 5-1/2 cups all-purpose
  flour
Caraway seeds and black
  cardamom seeds

1 cup milk
1/4 cup butter
2 eggs
Melted butter or egg

In large bowl, combine sugar, salt, yeast and 1-1/2 cups flour. In 1-quart saucepan, heat milk and butter until very warm. With mixer at low speed, gradually beat liquid into dry ingredients. At medium speed, beat 2 minutes, occasionally scraping bowl, with rubber spatula. Beat in eggs and about 1/2 cup flour to make a thick batter; continue beating 2 minutes. Stir in flour (2 to 2-1/2 cups) to make a soft dough. On lightly floured surface, knead dough until smooth and elastic, about 10 minutes. Shape dough into ball. Turn in greased large bowl to grease top. Cover; let rise in warm place until doubled, about 1 hour.

Punch down dough. Transfer to lightly floured surface; cut in half; cover; let rest 15 minutes.

Cut each half into 12 pieces; shape into balls and small loaves. Place 2 inches apart on greased cookie sheets. Cover; let rise until doubled, about 30 minutes. Preheat oven to 400 °F. Brush with melted butter or egg glaze. Sprinkle with caraway and cardamom seeds if you like. Bake 10 minutes or until golden.

Vienna rolls: Shape one half of dough into oval balls, tapering ends slightly. Place 2-inches apart on greased cookie sheet. Cover; let rise until doubled. With sharp, floured knife, slash lengthwise halfway through center of each roll. Beat 1 egg white with 1 tablespoon water until frothy; brush egg-white mixture over rolls. Sprinkle with caraway seeds.

Knots: Divide one half of dough into 6 equal pieces. Roll each piece into 6-inch long rope shape. Carefully tie each rope into a knot. Arrange on greased cookie sheet. Brush with melted butter. Cover let rise until doubled.

Crescents: Roll one half of dough into 9-inch circle. Cut circle into 12 wedges; brush with melted butter. Roll up each wedge toward point; place wedges on lightly greased cookie sheet. Curve ends. Cover with towel; let crescents rise until doubled.

Psies: Shape one half of dough into 6 balls. Place on greased cookie sheet. Flatten slightly. With scissors, make six 1/4-inch deep cuts in edge of each ball. Brush lightly with egg glaze; sprinkle with cardamom seed. Let rise until dough is doubled. Serves 8-12.

## Cheese Almond Bread

3-1/2 teaspoons sugar
2 teaspoons salt
2 packages active dry
  yeast
4 cups all-purpose flour
1/2 cup butter or margarine

1 cup milk
2 eggs
1 pound muenster cheese,
  shredded
1 tablespoon whole blanched almonds

In large bowl, combine sugar, salt, yeast and 1 cup flour. In 1-quart saucepan over low heat, heat butter and milk until very warm. With mixer at very low speed, gradually beat liquid into dry ingredients until just mixed. Increase speed to medium; beat two minutes, occasionally scraping bowl. Beat in 1 cup flour or enough to make a thick batter; continue beating 2 minutes, occasionally scraping bowl. With spoon, stir in enough additional flour (about 2 cups) to make a soft dough.

Turn dough onto lightly floured surface and knead until smooth and elastic, about 10 minutes, adding more flour while kneading, if necessary. Shape dough into ball; cover with bowl and let dough rest 15 minutes for easier shaping.

Meanwhile, reserve 1 egg white. In large bowl, thoroughly combine remaining eggs with cheese and set aside. Grease 9-inch cake pan. On lightly floured surface, with lightly floured rolling pin, roll dough into a 24x6 rectangle. Lengthwise along center of dough, shape cheese mixture into cylinder. Fold dough over filling, making about 1 to 1-1/2-inch overlap; pinch seam to seal. Place roll, seam side down, in pan to make a crescent moon or ring, overlapping ends slightly; pinch ends together to seal. Cover with towel; let rest in warm place 10 minutes.

Preheat oven to 375 °F. Brush loaf with reserved egg white. Garnish top with almonds. Bake 1 hour or until golden and bread sounds hollow when lightly tapped. Remove bread from pan immediately; let stand 15 minutes for easier cutting. Cut bread into wedges. Serves 8-10.

## Sesame Bread

3 tablespoons sugar
1 tablespoon salt
2 packages active dry
  yeast
6 cups all-purpose flour

2 cups water
1/4 cup butter or margarine
Milk
1 egg, slightly beaten
1/4 cup sesame seed

In large bowl, combine sugar, salt, yeast and 2 cups flour. In 2-quart saucepan over low heat, heat water, butter and 1 cup milk until very warm. With mixer at low speed, gradually beat liquid into dry ingredients until just mixed. Increase speed to medium;

beat 2 minutes, occasionally scraping bowl. Beat in egg and 1/2 cup flour or enough to make thick batter; continue beating 2 minutes at medium speed, occasionally scraping bowl. With wooden spoon, stir in enough additional flour (about 3 cups) to make a soft dough.

Turn dough onto lightly floured surface; knead until smooth and elastic, about 10 minutes, adding more flour while kneading, if needed. Shape into ball; cover with bowl; let rest 15 minutes. Grease two 9-inch round cake pans.

Cut dough in half; with fingers, press into pans evenly. Cover with towel; let rise in warm place until doubled, about 40 minutes.

Preheat oven to 350 °F. Brush loaves with milk; sprinkle with sesame seed. Bake 40 minutes or until golden and loaves sound hollow when tapped with fingers. Remove from pans; cool. Serves 15.

# DESSERTS

# Profiteroles

*-French-*
*Choux paste:*
*1/2 cup unsalted butter*
*1 cup water*
*1/4 teaspoon salt*

*1 cup all-purpose flour*
*4 eggs*

*Vanilla Pastry Cream:*
*3/4 cup sugar*
*1/4 cup all-purpose flour*
*3 egg yolks*

*1/4 teaspoon salt*
*1-1/2 cups milk*
*1-1/2 teaspoons vanilla extract*

*Chocolate Sauce:*
*1/2 pound bittersweet*
  *chocolate*
*2 cups milk*

*1/3 cup confectioners' sugar*

This a Turkish version of profiteroles. Many dessert shops in Turkey offer this popular dessert.

Choux paste: Grease 2 large cookie sheets. In 2-quart saucepan over medium heat, heat butter, water and salt until butter mixture boils. Remove from heat. Add flour all at once. With wooden spoon, vigorously stir until mixture forms a ball and leaves side of pan. Preheat oven to 375 °F. Add eggs to flour mixture, one at a time, mixing well after each addition, until smooth. Cool mixture slightly. Using teaspoon and rubber spatula, drop batter onto cookie sheets in small mounds, 2-inches apart, swirling top of each. Bake 50 minutes. Remove from the oven. Cool, prepare filling (Vanilla Pastry Cream), cover and chill. When puffs are cool, slice top off each. Fill each shell with chilled Vanilla Pastry Cream; replace top. Prepare chocolate sauce. Place 3 to 4 puffs on small plates, pour slightly warm chocolate sauce over the puffs and serve any excess separately. Serves 8-10.

Vanilla Pastry Cream: In medium saucepan, combine 3/4 cup sugar, 1/4 cup all-purpose flour and 1/4 teaspoon salt; stir in 1-1/2 cups milk. Over medium heat, cook, stirring, until mixture thickens and boils, about 10 minutes; boil 1 minute. In small bowl with fork, beat 3 egg yolks slightly; beat small amount of milk mixture into yolks; slowly pour egg mixture back into milk mixture, stirring. Cook over medium-low heat, stirring until mixture thickens and coats spoon well, about 8 minutes (do not boil). To check thickness, lift metal spoon from mixture and hold up 15 seconds; spoon should not show through mixture. Remove from heat; stir in 1-1/2 teaspoons vanilla extract. Cover surface with plastic wrap; chill well, about two hours.

Chocolate Sauce: In 2-quart saucepan, over low heat, melt chocolate and 1/3 cup confectioners' sugar and 2 cups milk, stirring constantly. Heat until smooth. Serve chocolate sauce slightly warm over vanilla cream puffs.

## Marble Cake

2 squares unsweetened chocolate
1-1/4 cups sugar
1/4 cup water
1 teaspoon vanilla extract
1/2 cup unsalted butter, softened
2 cups all-purpose flour
3/4 cup evaporated milk

3 eggs
2 teaspoons double-acting
  baking powder
1 teaspoon orange extract
1/2 teaspoon salt
1/2 teaspoon baking soda
Confectioners' sugar

Preheat oven to 350 °F. Grease generously 9-inch springform pan. In 1-quart saucepan over very low heat, melt chocolate and 1/4 cup sugar with water, stirring. Stir in vanilla; cool. Into large bowl, measure 1 cup sugar and all ingredients except chocolate mixture and confectioners' sugar. With mixer at low speed, beat until well mixed, constantly scraping bowl; at high speed, beat 5 minutes, scraping bowl occasionally. Remove 2-1/2 cups batter. Beat chocolate mixture into remaining batter; alternately spoon plain and chocolate batters into pan. With knife, cut through batter a few times, then bake 55 to 60 minutes; top will be cracked. Cool in pan on rack 10 minutes; remove sides of pan and cool cake on rack. Sprinkle top of cooled cake lightly with some confectioners' sugar. Serves 12.

## Chocolate Pecan Pound Cake

1-1/4 cups all-purpose flour
3/4 teaspoon baking powder
1/4 teaspoon salt
3/4 cup unsalted butter or
  margarine, softened
3/4 cup packed light brown sugar

1 teaspoon vanilla extract
3 eggs
3/4 cup chopped pecans, toasted,
  cooled and lightly floured
2 cups chocolate mini morsels, divided
Chopped pecans (optional)

In small bowl, combine flour, baking powder and salt. In large mixer bowl, cream butter, brown sugar and vanilla for 2 minutes. Add eggs, one at a time, beating well after each addition. Stir in lightly floured toasted pecans and 1-1/2 cups mini morsels. Spoon into greased 9x5 inch loaf pan. Bake in preheated 325 °F oven for 55 to 60 minutes or until wooden pick inserted in center comes out clean. Cool in pan for 20 minutes. Remove from pan; cool completely on wire rack. In small heavy saucepan over low heat, melt remaining morsels; drizzle over cake. Sprinkle with additional pecans. Serves 8.

## Deluxe Raisin Cake-Üzümlü Kek

*-Turkish-*
*3 cups all-purpose flour*
*1 teaspoon baking powder*
*1/2 teaspoon salt*
*2 cups sugar*
*1 cup unsalted butter, softened*
*3 teaspoons vanilla extract*
*4 eggs*

*3/4 cup milk*
*1 cup seedless raisins or*
*chocolate mini morsels,*
*lightly floured*

Preheat oven to 325 °F. In small bowl, combine flour, baking powder and salt; set aside. In large mixer bowl, beat sugar, butter and vanilla extract until creamy. Beat in eggs, one at a time, beating well after each addition. Gradually beat in flour mixture alternately with milk. In small cup, lightly flour raisins, (this process prevents raisins from sinking to the bottom of the pan). Stir in raisins. Pour into greased and floured 10-inch cake pan or fluted cake pan. Bake 70 to 80 minutes or until wooden pick inserted comes out clean. Cool in pan 15 minutes. Remove from pan and cool completely. Serves to: 6

## Valentine's Walnut Raisin Cake

*1-1/2 cups all-purpose flour*
*1/2 teaspoon baking powder*
*1/4 teaspoon salt*
*1 cup sugar*
*1/2 cup unsalted butter, softened*
*1-1/2 teaspoons vanilla extract*

*2 eggs*
*1/3 cup milk*
*1 cup seedless raisins,*
*lightly floured*
*1 cup chopped walnuts,*
*lightly floured*

Preheat oven to 325 °F. In small bowl, combine flour, baking powder and salt; set aside. In large mixer bowl, beat sugar, butter and vanilla extract until creamy. Beat in eggs, one at a time, beating well after each addition. Gradually beat in flour mixture alternately with milk. Stir in floured walnuts and raisins. Pour into greased and floured heart shaped pan.

Bake 70 to 80 minutes or until wooden pick inserted in center of cake comes out clean. Cool in pan 15 minutes. Remove from pan and cool completely. Serves to: 6

# Kahlua Swirl Cake

**Streusel Filling:**
1/3 cup brown sugar
1/3 cup chopped pecans
1/4 teaspoon cinnamon
1/4 teaspoon mace

**Cake:**
2 cups sifted all-purpose flour
1 teaspoon baking powder
3/4 teaspoon baking soda
3/4 teaspoon salt
1/2 teaspoon mace
1/2 cup unsalted butter, softened
1-1/4 cups granulated sugar

**Kahlua Glaze:**
3/4 cup sifted, powdered sugar
2 tablespoons unsalted butter, softened
1 tablespoon Kahlua

2 eggs
1 teaspoon vanilla
3/4 cup sour cream
3/4 cup Kahlua
Kahlua Glaze
Pecan halves
Streusel filling

Streusel Filling: Mix 1/3 cup packed brown sugar, 1/3 cup chopped pecans, 1/4 teaspoon cinnamon and mace.

Grease and flour 9-inch fluted tube pan. Prepare Streusel filling. Preheat oven 350 °F. Resift flour with baking powder, soda, salt and mace. In large bowl, combine butter, sugar, eggs and vanilla. Beat 2 minutes on medium speed. On lowest speed, blend in flour alternately with sour cream and Kahlua. Turn 1/3 batter into prepared pan. Cover with 1/2 Streusel filling, an additional 1/3 batter and remaining Streusel. Top with remaining batter. Bake on rack below oven center for 45 minutes or until golden brown. Remove; let stand 10 minutes. Invert on cake rack; cool until lukewarm. Remove pan. Spoon on Kahlua Glaze. Garnish with pecan halves.

Kahlua Glaze: Combine 3/4 cup sifted powdered sugar, 2 tablespoons softened butter and 1 tablespoon Kahlua; beat until smooth. Spoon over top of lukewarm cake. Serves 8.

# Deluxe Almond Cake with Chocolate

7 ounce almond paste
7 ounce granulated sugar
7 ounce unsalted butter, softened
Almond or fresh fruit slices
  to garnish

3 medium eggs
1/2 cup of cake flour
Pinch salt
Chocolate, melted
  for topping

Blend almond paste, sugar, and salt thoroughly in electric mixer at slow speed. Add butter gradually until well-mixed. On high speed, add eggs one at a time, mix until light and fluffy. Remove bowl from mixer. Fold in flour until just blended in. Grease and flour 10-inch pan and pour in batter. Bake at 325 °F for 40 minutes or until golden and inserted wooden pick comes out clean. Frost with melted chocolate; garnish with almond slices and cherries or with fresh fruit slices. For frosting, you can use white chocolate if you like. Serves 6.

# Rum Cake

2-1/4 cups cake flour
1-1/2 cups sugar
3/4 cup shortening
3/4 cup milk
3 eggs
2-1/2 teaspoons double-acting
Baking powder

1 teaspoon salt
1 teaspoon vanilla extract
1/2 teaspoon almond extract
1/2 cup Rum

Rum Glaze:
1 stick butter
1/4 cup water
1 cup granulated sugar
1/2 cup Rum

Chocolate Glaze Topping:
4-ounce semisweet chocolate
1 teaspoon unsalted butter

Preheat oven to 375 °F. Prepare fluted tube pan; first grease and then flour. Into large bowl, measure all ingredients. With mixer at low speed, beat until well mixed, constantly scraping bowl with rubber spatula. Increase speed to medium; beat 5 minutes, occasionally scraping bowl. Pour batter into prepared cake pan, smoothing top with rubber spatula. Cut through batter with knife to remove any air bubbles. Bake 25 minutes or until wooden pick inserted deep into center comes out clean. Cool for 10 minutes. Spoon and brush Rum Glaze evenly over cake, allowing cake to absorb the glaze. When cake is cooled, drizzle with Chocolate Glaze Topping; sprinkle with nuts.

Rum Glaze: Melt butter in saucepan. Stir in water and sugar. Boil 5 minutes. Remove from heat; stir in rum.

Chocolate Glaze Topping: Melt chocolate and butter together over very low heat in heavy saucepan. Serves 6-8.

# Pecan Pie

*Piecrust:*
*1-1/2 cups all-purpose flour*
*1/2 teaspoon salt*
*1-1/2 tablespoons sugar (optional)*
*Butter to brush pie plate*

*1/2 cup vegetable shorthening*
*3 to 4 tablespoons cold water,*
*   more if needed*

*Pecan pie:*
*1 (9-inch) unbaked piecrust*
*3 eggs*
*1 cup dark corn syrup*
*1/2 cup sugar*

*1/4 cup unsalted butter or margarine,*
*   melted*
*1 teaspoon vanilla extract*
*1-1/2 cups pecan halves*

You can use ready made pie crust or make one from scratch. For 2-piecrust, double the ingredients.

Preparing piecrust:. Sift four and salt into bowl. Add and cut shortening into flour mixture with 2 round-bladed table knives or pastry blender. With your fingertips, rub shortening into flour until mixture forms coarse crumbs, lifting and crumbling mixture to help aerate it. Sprinkle water over mixture, 1 tablespoon at a time, and mix lightly with fork. When crumbs are moist enough to start sticking together press dough lightly into ball, wrap it tightly, and chill until firm, about 30 minutes. Brush pie plate with melted butter. On lightly floured surface with lightly floured rolling pin, roll pastry into a round 2-inches larger than top of pie plate. Gently lift edge of dough with your fingertips, and press it well into bottom and up side of pie plate. Press to seal any cracks in dough. With kitchen scissors or sharp knife, trim pastry edges, leaving a 1-inch overhang. Fold under excess dough to make thicker edge. Flute edge of pastry shell; press your thumbs together diagonally into edge to make a ridge. Continue around edge in this way until fluting is completed. Prick bottom of pastry shell with fork to prevent air bubbles from forming during cooking. Chill until firm, about 15 minutes.

Preparing Pecan Pie: Preheat oven to 350 °F. In medium bowl with wire whisk or hand beater, beat eggs well. Beat in corn syrup, sugar, butter or margarine and vanilla extract until well blended. Arrange pecan halves in single layer in bottom of piecrust. Pour egg mixture over the pecans in piecrust being careful not to disturb nuts. Bake pie 1 hour or until knife inserted about 1-inch from edge comes out clean. Cool. Serves 8.

# Prune and Apricot Pie

1 (9-inch) baked piecrust (page 144)
Water
1 (12-ounce) package pitted prunes
  (about 2 cups)
1 cup dried apricots
1/4 cup chopped walnuts

3 tablespoons cornstarch
1/4 cup sugar
1 tablespoon finely grated
  lemon peel
1 teaspoon ground cinnamon
1/8 teaspoon salt

Prepare piecrust. Bake piecrust as follows: Heat oven to 400 °F. Heat metal baking sheet in oven. Line pastry shell with double thickness of aluminum foil, pushing well into bottom. Half-fill with dried beans (weighing down with aluminium foil filled with beans will help pie dough to keep its shape during baking). Bake on baking sheet until set and rim starts to brown, about 15 minutes. Remove foil and beans, discard them and reduce oven temperature to 375 F. Bake, 5 to 10 minutes longer; cool.

Preheat oven to 375 °F. In 2-quart saucepan over-high heat, heat 3 cups water, prunes and apricots to boiling; reduce heat to low and simmer 15 minutes or until fruits are tender. Meanwhile, spread walnuts on cookie sheet; toast in oven 8 minutes until lightly browned. In cup, blend cornstarch and 1/2 cup water; gradually stir into simmering fruit and cook, stirring constantly, until thickened. Stir in sugar, lemon peel, cinnamon and salt. Pour mixture into piecrust. Sprinkle with walnuts. Cool. Serves 8.


# Apple Pie

Pastry 2-crust pie (page 144)
2/3 to 3/4 cup sugar
2 tablespoons all-purpose flour
1/2 teaspoon ground cinnamon
1/4 teaspoon ground nutmeg
1/2 teaspoon grated lemon peel

1 to 2 teaspoons lemon juice
6 to 7 cups thinly sliced, peeled
  and cored cooking apples
  (2 pounds)
Margarine
Milk

Prepare pastry, double ingredients to make 2 crusts. Roll out half of pastry and line 9-inch pie plate. In small bowl, combine sugar (amount depends on tartness of apples) and next five ingredients. Place half of thinly sliced apples in piecrust; sprinkle with half of sugar mixture. Top with rest of apples, then rest of sugar mixture. Dot the filling with butter or margarine. Preheat oven to 425 °F. Roll out remaining pastry for top crust and using a floured leaf-shaped cookie cutter, cut out design. Place crust over pie; trim edges. Fold pastry overhang under then bring up over pie-plate rim. Pinch to form a high edge then make your choice of decorative edge. For a golden glaze, brush top crust (not the edge) lightly with some milk. Bake pie for 40 to 50 minutes or until crust is golden. Serves 6.

# Banana Cream Pie

2 cups Graham cookie crumbs
1/2 cup sugar
1/3 cup all-purpose flour
1/4 teaspoon salt
2-1/4 cups milk

4 egg yolks
1 tablespoon unsalted butter
2 teaspoons vanilla extract
1 cup heavy cream
4 medium bananas

Garnishing:
1/3 cup apple jelly
1 medium banana

1 lemon
Grated lemon peels

Prepare crumb crust as directed on label. Press it on the side of 9-inch pie pan and bake in 350 °F oven for 8 to 10 minutes; cool, set aside. In 2-quart saucepan with spoon, mix sugar, flour and salt. Stir in milk until smooth. Over medium heat, cook mixture, stirring constantly, until mixture is thickened and begins to boil (about 10 minutes). Boil 1 minute. Remove immediately from heat and set aside. In cup with wire whisk, beat egg yolks with small amount of hot milk mixture. Slowly pour egg mixture into saucepan, stirring rapidly to prevent lumping. Over low heat, cook stirring constantly, until very thick (do not boil) and mixture mounds when dropped from spoon. Remove from heat; stir in butter and vanilla. Cover surface of filling with plastic wrap; refrigerate until cool, about 2 hours. Peel and slice 3 medium bananas over bottom of cookie crust; top with filling; chill until set, about 2 hours. Spread whipped cream evenly on top-edge of pie. To garnish, grate peel of 1 lemon; sprinkle around top-edge of pie. Cut lemon in half and squeeze juice into bowl. Into juice, peel and slice 1 large banana; toss to coat; drain on paper towels. Arrange banana slices in center of top of pie. In 1-quart saucepan over low heat, heat 1/3 cup apple jelly until just melted; brush over banana slices. Chill. Serves 8.

# Peach Pie

1 cup sugar
1/4 cup cornstarch
1/8 teaspoon salt
3 tablespoons unsalted butter

Pastry for 2-crust pie (page 144)
10 cups sliced peaches
    (about 5 pounds)

In medium bowl, combine sugar, cornstarch, cinnamon and salt; set aside. Prepare pastry, increase double crust-ingredients to make 2 crusts; cut off one-fourths of pastry into 17x13 rectangle. Use to line 12x8 baking dish. Add peaches to dish; dot with butter; sprinkle with sugar mixture. Preheat oven to 425 °F. Roll remaining pastry into 10x6-inch rectangle; cut into six 1-inch-wide strips; place the strips crosswise over the peach filling, twisting them. Make a high, fluted edge. Bake 50 minutes or until filling is bubbly and crust is golden brown. Let stand 15 minutes, then serve warm. Or cool to serve cold. Serves 10.

# Lemon Meringue

1 (9-inch) baked piecrust
  (page 144)
1/3 cup corn starch
Sugar
Salt
1-1/2 cups warm water
1 lemon peel, grated
1/2 cup lemon juice

4 eggs separated
1 tablespoon unsalted butter
  or margarine
4 egg white for meringue topping

Baked piecrust: Prepare piecrust as directed on (page 144). Preheat oven to 400 °F. With fork, prick bottom and side of crust in many places to prevent puffing during baking. Heat metal baking sheet in oven. Line pastry shell with a double thickness of aluminum foil, pushing well into the bottom. Half-fill with dried beans (weighing down with aluminum foil filled with beans will help piecrust to keep its shape during baking). Bake on baking sheet until set and rim starts to brown, about 15 minutes. Remove foil and beans and reduce oven temperature to 375 °F. Bake, 5 to 10 minutes longer. Cool.

Lemon Meringue pie: Into 2-quart saucepan, measure cornstarch, 1 cup sugar and 1/8 teaspoon salt; stir together. Stir in water, lemon peel and juice; cook over medium heat, stirring, until mixture boils; remove from heat. In small bowl with wire whisk or spoon, beat egg yolks; then stir in small amount of hot sauce. Slowly pour egg mixture into sauce, stirring rapidly to prevent lumping. Return to heat; cook, stirring, until mixture is thick (do not boil). Add butter or margarine to thickened mixture and stir until melted and thoroughly blended. Pour mixture into pie crust.

4-egg Meringue Topping: Preheat oven to 400 °F. Have egg whites at room temperature. Be sure bowl and beaters are completely free of fat. In small bowl with a mixer at high speed, beat egg whites and salt until soft peaks form. At high speed, sprinkle in sugar, 2 tablespoons at a time, beating after each addition until sugar is dissolved. Rub a bit of meringue between fingers; if it does not feel grainy, sugar is dissolved. Whites should stand in stiff, glossy peaks. With back of spoon, spread meringue over filling; seal to pie crust all around edge. Swirl up points to make attractive top. Bake 10 minutes or until golden. Cool away from drafts. Serves 6.

# Cake Milano

8 eggs
2 cups sugar
2-3/4 cups cake flour
1 cup milk
1 cup unsalted butter
  or margarine

3 teaspoons double-acting
Baking powder
1 teaspoon salt
1 teaspoon vanilla extract
Filling
Frosting

Filling:
8 egg yolks
1-1/4 cups sugar
1/2 cup butter
1 cup chopped dark seedless
  raisins

1 (4-ounce) can shredded coconut
1 cup pecan halves
1 cup candied red cherries, chopped
1/3 cup bourbon

Frosting:
1-1/2 cups sugar
1 tablespoon dark corn syrup
1/3 cup water

1/2 teaspoon salt
1 teaspoon vanilla extract

Preheat oven to 375 °F. Separate eggs, placing 6 whites in large bowl, 2 whites in small bowl and all the yolks in 2-quart saucepan. Grease two 9-inch round cake pans; line bottoms of cake pans with waxed paper; grease. In large bowl with mixer at high speed, beat egg whites until soft peaks form. Beating at high speed, sprinkle in 1 cup sugar, 2 tablespoons at a time. Beat until stiff peaks form. In another large bowl at low speed, mix flour, next 5 ingredients and 1 cup sugar. At medium speed, beat 4 minutes; fold in whites.

Pour into cake pans; bake 35 minutes. Cool pans on wire racks 10 minutes; remove from pans; discard paper; cool. Prepare filling. Cut each layer in half horizontally; assemble 4-layer cake with filling. Prepare frosting; frost cake.

Filling: Into 8 egg yolks, stir 1-1/4 cups sugar and 1/2 cup butter. Over medium heat, cook, stirring until slightly thickened, about 5 minutes. Stir in one 4-ounce can shredded coconut, 1 cup pecan halves, chopped, 1 cup candied red cherries, chopped, 1 cup dark seedless raisins, chopped and 1/3 cup bourbon.

Frosting: In 1-quart saucepan over medium heat, heat 1 1/2 cups sugar, 1 tablespoon dark corn syrup, 1/3 cup water and 1/2 teaspoon salt to boiling. Boil, without stirring, to 240°F on candy thermometer. Remove from heat. With mixer at high speed, beat reserved 2 egg whites until soft peaks form. Pour syrup in thin stream into whites, beating constantly. Add 1 teaspoon vanilla extract and continue beating until very thick. Serves 12-14.

# Coconut Cake from Newport Beach

2-1/4 cups cake flour
1-1/2 cups sugar
3/4 cup shortening
3/4 cup milk
3 eggs
2-1/2 teaspoons double-
  acting baking powder
1 teaspoon salt
1 teaspoon vanilla extract

Custard Filling
Meat from 1 medium coconut,
  shredded, (2 to 4 cups meat)
Frosting
Candied orange slices
  for garnish

Custard Filling:
4 egg yolks
2 cups milk
1/2 cup sugar
1/3 cup cornstarch
3 tablespoons orange-flavor
  liqueur

Frosting:
1-1/4 cups light corn syrup
2 egg whites
1/8 teaspoon salt
1 teaspoon vanilla extract

Preheat oven to 375 °F. Grease and flour two 9-inch round cake pans. In large bowl with mixer at low speed, beat first 8 ingredients until well mixed, constantly scraping bowl. Beat at medium speed 5 minutes, occasionally scraping bowl. Pour into pans; bake 25 to 30 minutes until wooden pick comes out clean. Cool in pans on wire racks 10 minutes; remove from pans and cool completely on racks.

Meanwhile, prepare custard filling. Custard Filling: In heavy, 2-quart saucepan with wire whisk, mix well 4 egg yolks, 2 cups milk, 1/2 cup sugar, 1/3 cup cornstarch and 3 tablespoons orange-flavor liqueur until well blended; then, over medium heat, cook, stirring constantly, until mixture thickens, about 10 minutes. Cover custard surface with waxed paper; refrigerate until well chilled, about 1-1/2 hours. Stir 1 cup shredded coconut into chilled custard filling.

Prepare frosting. Frosting: In 1-quart saucepan over medium heat, heat corn syrup to boiling; remove from heat. In large bowl with mixer at high speed, beat egg whites until foamy; add salt and continue beating just until soft peaks form. Slowly pour in hot syrup, beating 6 to 8 minutes until the mixture is fluffy and peaks form when beater is raised. Beat in vanilla extract.

With sharp knife, cut each cake horizontally in half. Place first layer on cake plate, cut side up; spread cake with 1/3 of filling. Repeat layering, ending with a cake layer, top side up.

Frost side and top of cake. Sprinkle side and top of cake with about 2 cups shredded coconut. Garnish top with candied orange slices. Refrigerate until serving time. Serves 14-16.

# The Concorde's Chocolate-Raspberry Dream Cake

2 cups all-purpose flour
1-3/4 cups sugar
3/4 cup cocoa powder
1-1/4 teaspoons baking soda
1 teaspoon salt

1/2 teaspoon baking powder
1-1/4 cups milk
3/4 cup butter
3 eggs
1 teaspoon vanilla

*Frosting:*
2 cups heavy whipping cream
1/2 cup powdered sugar
2 tablespoons unsweetened
  cocoa powder
6 tablespoons raspberry jam

In large mixing bowl, place all the cake ingredients. Beat with electric mixer on low speed until well mixed, then beat for five minutes at high speed. Pour batter into pans. Stagger pans on 2 oven racks so that no pan is directly above another. Bake 20 to 30 minutes or until wooden pick placed in center comes out clean. Cool pans on wire racks for 10 minutes; remove layers from pans and cool them on wire racks for two hours.

In chilled mixing bowl, beat whipping cream until fairly stiff. Add powdered sugar and cocoa powder and beat until cream has stiff peaks. Place one cake layer on a platter; spread half the raspberry jam and some of the whipped cream on top. Repeat with next layer; then frost top and sides with shaved chocolate curls or garnish with raspberries if desired. Serves 6.

# Leman's Rich Chestnut-Chocolate Dome

*-Turkish-*
2 (18 oz.) can Turkish candied
  chestnuts in heavy syrup
1/2 cup sliced blanched almonds
1/2 teaspoon vanilla extract

1 cup Graham-cracker crumbs
1-1/2 cup milk
1/4 pound chocolate

Reserve 4 to 5 tablespoons sweet syrup from chestnuts, discard the rest. With fork, break sweet cooked chestnuts into small pieces. Reserve 8 to 10 whole pieces. In small saucepan melt chocolate with 1 cup milk, stirring until thickened; cover and set aside.

In large bowl, mix heated milk, Graham-cracker crumbs until well blended in; add sweet chestnut pieces and 4 to 5 tablespoons sweet syrup, 2 tablespoons warm chocolate sauce and vanilla extract, mix gently. Finally add whole chestnut pieces and make a chestnut ball. Place chestnut ball on serving plate, make a dome shape by pressing on top gently. Cover chestnut dome with heavy chocolate sauce, cool and garnish with sliced almonds. Serves 4-6.

# German Chocolate Cake

*-German-*

1 package sweet cooking
  chocolate
2 cups all-purpose flour
1 teaspoon baking soda
1/4 teaspoon salt
1 cup unsalted butter
  or margarine, softened

2 cups sugar
4 eggs, separated
1 teaspoon vanilla extract
 1 cup buttermilk
 Classic coconut-pecan filling
   and frosting, pecan halves
   (optional)

*Classic Coconut-Pecan Filling and frosting:*
1 can (12-ounces) evaporated milk (1-1/2 cups)
1-1/2 cups sugar
4 egg yolks, lightly beaten
3/4 cup (1-1/2 sticks) butter or margarine
1-1/2 teaspoons vanilla extract
2 cups flaked coconut
1-1/2 cups chopped pecans

Preheat oven to 350 °F. Line bottoms of three 9-inch round cake pans with waxed paper. In large microwave safe bowl, combine chocolate and 1/2 cup water. Microwave on high 1-1/2 to 2 minutes, or until chocolate is almost melted. Stir until chocolate is completely melted.

In small bowl, combine flour, baking soda and salt; set aside. In large bowl with electric mixer at medium speed, beat butter and sugar until light and fluffy. Add egg yolks, one at a time, beating well after each addition. Stir in melted chocolate and vanilla. Add flour mixture alternately with buttermilk, beating well after each addition until smooth.

In medium-sized bowl with electric mixer at high speed, beat egg whites until stiff peaks form. Gently stir into chocolate batter. Pour batter into prepared pans. Bake 30 minutes or until cake springs back when lightly touched with finger. Immediately run spatula between cake and sides of pans; cool in pans 15 minutes. Remove from pans; peel off waxed paper and cool completely on wire racks.

Meanwhile prepare classic coconut-pecan filling and frosting; Classic coconut-pecan filling and frosting: In medium sized saucepan, combine milk, sugar, egg yolks, butter and vanilla. Place over medium heat and cook about 12 minutes or until mixture thickens and is golden brown, stirring constantly. Remove from heat. Stir in coconut and pecans. With wooden spoon or electric mixer at medium speed, beat until cool and of spreading consistency.

Spread the frosting between layers and over top of cake. Garnish top of cake with pecan halves. This delicate cake will have a flat, slightly sugary top crust that tends to crack. This is normal and the frosting will cover it up. Makes 4-1/4 cups. Serves 12.

# Banana Roll Cake-Muzlu Rulo Pasta

*-Turkish-*
*3/4 cup all-purpose flour*
*1 teaspoon double-acting*
*  baking powder*
*1/2 teaspoon salt*
*4 eggs, separated*
*Sugar*

*1/2 teaspoon vanilla extract*
*Confectioners sugar*
*Vanilla filling (page 146)*
*3 bananas, peeled, cut 3-inch*
*  long pieces*
*Fresh fruit slices*

Preheat oven to 375 °F. Grease 15x10 jelly-roll pan; line with waxed paper. In small bowl, combine flour, baking powder and salt. In another small bowl with mixer at high speed, beat whites into soft peaks; gradually sprinkle in 1/3 cup sugar, beating until sugar is completely dissolved and stiff peaks form. In large bowl at high speed, beat egg yolks until thick and lemon-colored; at same speed, gradually sprinkle in 1/2 cup sugar then vanilla extract. Sprinkle flour mixture over yolks; add beaten whites. With rubber spatula, gently fold mixture to blend thoroughly.

Lay out waxed paper on pan. Spread batter in pan; bake 15 minutes or until top springs back when lightly touched with finger. Meanwhile, sprinkle cloth towel with 1/3 cup confectioners' sugar. Immediately invert hot cake onto towel; gently remove waxed paper and cut off crisp edges of cake, if you like. While still warm, carefully roll up cake and towel from narrow end.

Cool cake completely on rack, then unroll and spread with vanilla filling and place 3-inch long banana pieces. Reroll without towel and sprinkle roll with confectioners' sugar. Garnish with sliced fresh fruits (banana, peach, kiwi slices). Serves 8.

# Eclair

*-French-*
*Choux paste (page 139)*
*Vanilla pastry cream (page 139)*

*Chocolate Glaze:*
*6 squares bittersweet chocolate*
*2 tablespoons butter*
*3/4 cup confectioners' sugar*
*3 tablespoons milk*

Preheat oven to 375 °F. Make choux paste as in profiterole recipe; drop by 1/4 cupfuls onto cookie sheet 2-inches apart, and in rows 6-inches apart, to make 10. Spread each mound into a slim rectangle, rounding edges. Bake 40 minutes or until lightly browned. Cut slit in side of each shell and bake 10 minutes longer. Turn off oven; dry shells in oven 10 minutes. Cool on rack. Meanwhile, prepare vanilla pastry.

Slice about 1/3 from top of each shell and fill bottom of shells with cream filling; replace tops. Start preparing chocolate glaze.

Chocolate Glaze: Over low heat, melt 4 squares bitter sweet chocolate and 2 tablespoons butter, stirring constantly. Stir in 3/4 cup confectioners' sugar and 3 tablespoons milk until smooth. Spread glaze on top. Refrigerate until serving time. Serves 10.

## Cream Puffs with Honey Glaze-Balli Badem

*-Turkish-*
*Choux paste and vanilla*
  *pastry cream (page 139)*
*2 tablespoons honey*
*1 cup sugar*

*1 cup water*
*1/2 teaspoon lemon juice*

Prepare choux paste and vanilla pastry filling. Form large cream puffs. After baking puffs, fill them with vanilla pastry cream. Cover with the top parts. In small saucepan boil honey, sugar, water and lemon juice until it is thickened, and golden. Ladle syrup over the cream puffs. Hot syrup immediately will turn to hard candy shells. Serves 12.

## Blueberry Cheese Cake

*-American-*
*1-1/2 cups shortbread cookie*
  *crumbs*
*2 tablespoons unsalted butter,*
  *melted*
*3 (8-ounce) packages cream*
  *cheese, softened*

*1 tablespoon vanilla extract*
*1 (14-ounce) can sweetened*
  *condensed milk*
*4 eggs*
*1 (8-ounce) container sour cream*

*Blueberry-Brandy Topping:*
*1 (1-pound) package frozen*
  *blueberries*
*1 cup water*
*3/4 cup sugar*

*1/2 cup brandy*
*1 tablespoon cornstarch*
*1/8 teaspoon salt*
*1 teaspoon lemon juice*

Preheat oven to 350 °F. Combine crumbs and butter; press firmly on bottom of 9-inch springform pan. In large mixer bowl, beat cheese until fluffy. Gradually beat in sweetened condensed milk until smooth. Beat in eggs, then sour cream and vanilla. Pour into prepared pan. Bake 50 to 55 minutes or until lightly browned around edge (center will be soft); cool. Chill; top with Blueberry-Brandy topping. You can also top with Morello cherries or quince preserves heated with brandy.

Blueberry-Brandy Topping: In small saucepan combine all ingredients. Over medium heat cook, stirring constantly, until mixture is thickened and boils; remove from heat; cool pour over cheese cake. Serves 6-8.

## Marbled Double Chocolate Cheese Cake Squares

*1/2 cup (1 stick) unsalted
  butter, softened
1 cup sugar, divided
1/4 teaspoon salt
1 cup all-purpose flour
1/4 cup cocoa*

*2 packages (8oz. each) cream
  cheese, softened
2 eggs
2 teaspoons vanilla extract
1/2 cup chocolate topping
1/4 cup chocolate chips*

Heat oven to 350 °F. Line 8- or 9-inch square baking pan with foil, extending edges over sides of pan. In small mixing bowl, beat butter, 1/2 cup sugar and salt until smooth. Stir together flour and cocoa; gradually add to butter mixture, beating until soft dough is formed. Press dough onto bottom of prepared pan. Beat cream cheese and remaining 1/2 cup sugar until smooth. Add eggs and vanilla; blend well. In separate bowl, mix one cup batter with topping, stirring until well blended. Pour 1 cup of topping flavored batter over dough. Stir melted chocolate into remaining flavored batter. Drop tablespoonfuls of reserved flavored batter over top; gently swirl with knife or spatula for marbled effect. Bake 35 to 40 minutes or until cheesecake is firm and slightly puffed. Cool completely in pan on wire rack; refrigerate. To serve, lift from pan using foil edges; cut into squares. Garnish as desired. About 20 squares. Serves 12.

## Crème Caramel

*-French-
6 eggs
3/4 cup sugar
2-1/2 teaspoons vanilla
  extract
2 cups milk*

*Caramel syrup:
1 cup water
2/3 cup sugar
1 teaspoon lemon juice*

This is the Turkish version of crème caramel. Heat 1 cup water, 2/3 cup sugar and lemon juice, over medium heat, until syrup thickened and brown. Remove from heat. Pour syrup into glass or aluminum custard cups. Place cups in deep baking pan. Meanwhile boil milk with vanilla extract over medium heat. Remove from heat. In electric mixer, mix sugar and 2 eggs and 4 egg yolks. Discard unused egg whites. Add vanilla-milk mixture to egg-sugar mixture gradually, stir quickly and thoroughly until egg mixture blended in completely. Pour mixture in cups; pour hot water in pan to within 1-inch of top of cups; bake at 350 °F for 50 minutes or until knife inserted in center comes out clean. Cool on wire racks; refrigerate; with knife loosen custard from cups and invert onto dessert plates, letting syrup run down sides onto plate. Serves 6.

# Fruit Cream Tarts

*-French-*
*Baked tart shells*
*1/4 cup sugar*
*2 tablespoons cornstarch*
*1/4 teaspoon salt*
*1 cup milk*
*1 egg*

*1 teaspoon vanilla extract*
*1/2 cup heavy or whipping cream,*
 *whipped*
*1 cup currant jelly*
*1 tablespoon water*

*Baked Tart Shells:*
*1-1/2 cups all-purpose flour*
*6 tablespoons unsalted butter*
*1/3 cup sugar*
*1/2 teaspoon vanilla extract*

*1/4 teaspoon salt*
*3 egg yolks*
*Butter to brush molds*

*Garnish:*
*whole or sliced strawberries, blueberries, raspberries, peach slices, apricot halves or mandarin-orange sections, drained.*

Prepare tart shells. Custard: In 2-quart saucepan, mix sugar, cornstarch and salt; stir in milk until smooth. Over medium heat, cook, stirring, until mixture boils; boil 1 minute.

In 1-cup measure with fork, beat egg slightly, then slowly stir in small amount of the hot sauce.

Slowly pour egg mixture into sauce, stirring rapidly to prevent lumping. Cook, stirring, until thickened (do not boil).

Cover with waxed paper and refrigerate. When the custard is cold (after about 40 minutes), stir in vanilla extract; then, with wire whisk, fold in whipped cream.

Spoon custard into shells. Top with fruit. If you like, in 1-quart saucepan, melt jelly and water; cool slightly; spoon over fruit. Refrigerate until jelly sets.

Baked Tart Shells: Sift flour onto work surface and make a well in center. Pound butter with rolling pin to soften it. Add sugar, softened butter, vanilla extract, salt and egg yolks into well. With your fingertips, work ingredients in the well until thoroughly mixed. Draw in flour with pastry scraper, then work flour into other ingredients with your fingers until coarse crumbs form.With your fingers, press crumbs firmly together to form a ball dough. If dough is sticky, work in a little more flour. Lightly flour work surface. Blend dough by pushing it away from you with hell of your hand, then gathering it up, until it is very smooth and peels away from work surface, 1-2 minutes. Shape dough into a ball, wrap it tightly, and chill until firm, about 30 minutes.

Melt butter, then brush 4 of the tart-dough molds with butter. Lightly flour work surface. Roll out 2/3 of the chilled tart-dough until 1/8-inch thick. Return remaining dough to refrigerator. Cut out 4 rounds with cookie cutter; they should be large enough to line the molds completely. With your thumb, press 1 round well into bottom and up side of a mold to form a neat pastry shell. Repeat same process for remaining rounds. Add dough trimmings to remaining 1/3 dough. Prick bottom of each pastry shell with fork to prevent air bubbles from forming during baking. Chill shells until firm, about 15 minutes. Heat oven to 400 F. Place metal baking sheet in oven to heat. Carefully line each pastry shell with a second mold, so that they keep their shape during baking. Bake on baking sheet in heated oven until set and rims start to brown, 6 to 8 minutes. Remove lining molds, and reduce oven temperature to 375 F. Continue baking shells until dough is thoroughly cooked and golden brown, 3 to 5 minutes longer. Unmold and transfer each pastry shell to wire rack to cool. Let molds cool. Roll out remaining dough, line molds, chill, and bake 4 more pastry shells in same way. Fill baked tart shells with chilled vanilla custard. Serves 8.

## Apple Strudel

*-German-*
*2 pounds tart cooking apples,*
  *thinly sliced*
*1/2 cup dark seedless raisins*
  *or currants*
*1/2 cup chopped walnuts*
  *or pecans*
*1/3 cup sugar*
*1/2 teaspoon ground cinnamon*
*1/4 teaspoon ground nutmeg*

*1/4 teaspoon salt*
*1 cup dry bread crumbs*
*1/2 pound phyllo (Strudel leaves)*
*1/2 cup unsalted butter or*
  *margarine, melted*

Grease 15-1/2 x 10-1/2" jelly roll pan. In large bowl, mix first 7 ingredients and 1/2 cup bread crumbs, set apple mixture aside. Cut two 25-inch lengths of waxed paper; overlap two long sides about 1/2-inch; fasten with cellophane tape.

On waxed paper, place one sheet of phyllo; brush with some butter then sprinkle with scant tablespoon of remaining bread crumbs. Preheat oven to 375 °F. Layer remaining sheets of phyllo to make an 18-inch square, brushing each sheet with butter and sprinkling with crumbs.

Evenly spoon apple mixture in a 12x4 row, leaving 3-inches of phyllo at each end. Fold ends over apples. Starting with edge by apples, roll phyllo jelly-roll fashion. Place roll in jelly-roll pan seam side down. Brush with melted butter. Bake 40 minutes or just until golden brown.

Remove cooked strudel from oven and allow to cool in jelly-roll pan on wire rack about 30 minutes. With sharp knife, cut strudel crosswise into individual serving pieces; serve warm or cold. Serves 8-10.

# Almond and Raspberry Tart

*-Austrian-*

*Almond Pastry Dough:*
1 lemon
1-1/2 cups whole blanched almonds
1 cup all-purpose flour, more if
  needed
1/2 teaspoon cinnamon
1 pinch of ground cloves
1/2 cup butter, more for tart pan

1 egg yolk
1/2 cup sugar
*Red Raspberry Filling:*
1-1/4 pints red raspberries
6 to 8 tablespoons sugar
1 to 2 tablespoons confectioners'
  sugar

Almond Pastry Dough: Grate zest from lemon onto a piece of parchment paper. Halve lemon and squeeze juice from 1 half, about 1-1/2 tablespoons. Put whole almonds in food processor, add half of flour and grind finely. Sift remaining flour onto work surface with cinnamon and cloves. Mix in ground almond, then make well. Pound butter to soften it. Add butter, egg yolk, sugar, salt, lemon juice, and zest into well. Using your fingertips, work ingredients in well until thoroughly mixed. Draw in flour, and work it into other ingredients until coarse crumbs form. Press dough into ball, adding little more flour if it is sticky. Lightly flour work surface. Blend dough by pushing it away from you with hell of your hand. Then gather it up with pastry scraper, and continue to blend until it is very smooth and peels away from work surface in one piece, 1 to 2 minutes. Shape into ball, wrap tightly, and chill until firm, 1 to 2 hours. While it is chilling, prepare filling.

Red Raspberry Filling: In large saucepan, cook red raspberries and sugar, stirring, until they form thick pulpy jam, 10 to 12 minutes. Set aside cool. With back of wooden spoon, press half of the fruit pulp through strainer, set over bowl, to remove seeds. Stir in remaining pulp, leaving seeds for texture.

Brush tart pan with melted butter. Lightly flour work surface; roll out 2/3 of dough into an 11-inch round. Rewrap and chill remaining dough.

Wrap dough around rolling pin, then drape it over pan. Gently lift edge of dough with one hand, and press it into bottom of tart pan with other hand. Overlap dough slightly inside pan rim. Roll rolling pin over top of pan, to cut excess dough. Reserve trimmings. With your thumbs, press dough evenly up side of tart pan to increase height of shell.

Spread filling over bottom of shell. Roll out remaining dough; trim to 6x12-inch rectangle. Reserve trimmings. Cut dough into twelve 1/2-inch strips with fluted pastry wheel. Carefully arrange half of strips from left to right across tart, about 3/4-inch apart. Turn tart 45° and arrange remaining strips diagonally over first strips to form a lattice effect. Cut excess of strips. Roll all dough trimmings into long cylinder, then roll out thinly. Using fluted pastry wheel, cut three to four 1/2-inch strips to go around edge of tart. Brush edge of tart with cold water. Arrange strips around edge, pressing with your fingertips. Chill until dough is firm, about 15 minutes.

Heat oven to 375 °F. Place metal baking sheet in oven to heat. Bake tart on baking sheet until pastry begins to brown, 15 minutes. Reduce oven temperature to 350 °F, and continue baking until tart is golden brown and just beginning to shrink from side of tart pan, 25 to 30 minutes longer. Transfer tart to wire rack, and let cool slightly. Set tart pan on bowl to loosen and remove side (if you are using 2-piece, bottom part removable tart pan). Slide tart from pan base onto wire rack, and let cool completely. Before serving, dust entire surface of tart with confectioners' sugar. Serves 6-8.

## Mincemeat Tart

*Pastry Dough:*
*2-1/2 cups flour*
*1-1/2 tablespoons sugar*
*1/2 teaspoon salt*
*6 tablespoons vegetable shortening*
*6 tablespoons unsalted butter, more*
  *tart pan*
*6 to 7 tablespoons cold water*
  *more if needed*
*1 egg plus 1/2 teaspoon salt for*
  *glaze*

*Mincemeat Filling:*
*1 medium tart apple*
*1 lemon*
*1 cup seedless grapes*
*1 tablespoon silvered almonds*
*1/4 teaspoon each ground cinnamon,*
  *nutmeg and allspice*
*1/2 cup each dark raisins and*
  *golden raisins*
*1 tablespoon candied orange peel,*
  *chopped*
*1/2 cup light brown sugar*
*3 tablespoons whiskey*

Pastry Dough: Sift flour, sugar, and salt into medium bowl. Cut chilled shortening and butter into pieces, and add to flour mixture; then cut into mixture with pastry blender or with 2 round-bladed table knives. Rub in mixture with your fingertips until mixture forms coarse crumbs, lifting and crumbling to help aerate it. Sprinkle water over mixture, 1 tablespoon at a time, and mix lightly with fork. Continue mixing with fork until crumbs are moist enough to start sticking together. Press dough lightly into ball, wrap it tightly, and chill until firm, about 30 minutes.

Brush pan with melted butter. Lightly flour work surface, and roll out 2/3 of dough into 12-inch round. Return remaining dough to refrigerator. Wrap dough around pin, and drape it over pan. Gently lift edge of dough with one hand, and press it well into bottom pan with other hand, pressing to seal any cracks. Overlap dough slightly inside rim of pan. Roll rolling pin over top of pan, pressing down to cut off excess dough. With your thumbs, press dough evenly up pan side to increase height of shell. Chill shell until firm, about 15 minutes. Meanwhile prepare filling.

Mincemeat Filling: Peel apple, and cut out stem ends. Halve apple, then scoop out core. Set each apple half cut-side down, and cut horizontally into 1/2-inch slices. Cut slices lenghtwise into 1/2-inch strips. Gather strips together and cut crosswise into cubes. Grate zest from lemon onto sheet of parchment paper. Halve lemon, and squeeze juice. With small knife, cut grapes lengthwise in half. Place apple, grapes, lemon zest and juice, candied orange peel, almonds, ground cinnamon, nutmeg, and allspice, dark and golden raisins, sugar and whiskey into medium bowl. Stir to combine. Spoon fresh mincemeat over bottom of pastry shell, and gently press it down with back of spoon.

Make egg glaze: Lightly beat egg with salt. Roll out remaining dough, until dough 10-1/2x10-1/2 inch square. Using knife, cut dough into 3/4-inch strips. Decorate the surface with strips by giving lattice effect. Brush ends of strips with cold water. With your finger tips, seal strips to pastry shell, pinching off overhanging ends. Brush lattice like top with egg glaze. Chill until firm, about 15 minutes. Heat oven to 350°F. Place baking sheet in oven to heat. Bake on metal baking sheet until lightly browned about 40-45 minutes. Let cool slightly on wire rack; set on bowl to loosen and remove side (if you are using 2-piece, bottom side removable tart pan). Serves 8.

## Mille Feuilles

*-French-*
*1 (8-ounce) package puff pastry*
*1/2 pint double cream*
*1/2 teaspoon allspice*

*1 bottle strawberry jam*
*Confectioners' sugar*
*Fruit*

Preheat oven to 425 °F. Cut puffy pastry in half and roll into two rectangles approximately 11x6-inch. Place on two damp baking trays and cook for 10-15 minutes until raised and golden brown. Allow to cool.

Whisk double cream with allspice until thick. Spread strawberry jam over one half of the pastry. Cover with fruit if desired, followed by the cream. Top with remaining pastry and sprinkle with confectioners' sugar. Serves 4.

# Baklava

*-Turkish-*

| | |
|---|---|
| *4 cups pistachios or walnuts* | *Sugar Syrup:* |
| *3 sticks (4-ounce each)* | *3-1/2 cups sugar* |
|   *unsalted butter* | *5 cups water* |
| *1 package phyllo sheets* | *1 teaspoon freshly grated* |
|   *or Turkish baklava dough* |   *lemon zest (optional)* |

In the Ottoman court kitchen, pastry making reached extraordinary heights. Baklava is probably the most famous example. In every region the Turks ruled during Ottoman times (Georgia, Tunisia, Greece, Syria and Slavic Macedonia), one will find some version of this type of dessert. If you walk into baklava-shops (Baklavaci) in Turkey, you will find great selection of baklava, other syruped desserts and candied chestnuts, pistachios and almond pastes with unique fresh flavors (Kestane sekeri, sam fistigi ve badem ezmesi).

A well-baked baklava must be crisp, light, and fluffy on top and soft inside; it must have a moist and nutty filling, a syrupy thin bottom crust and perhaps most important, it must balance the taste of nuts, butter and sugar. Of course, it must be sweet.

Using phyllo type-dough we can only imitate the original baklava's texture and softness inside. Turkish baklava makers use original baklava dough which is similar to phyllo dough. Since phyllo type-dough is readily available, measurements are given in this recipe are for phyllo type dough.

Preheat oven to 350 °F. Coarsely grind pistachios; place in small bowl. Brush 9x13-inch baking dish with melted butter. Unfold phyllo dough so it lays flat, then cover to prevent it from drying out. Line dish with half of the phyllo sheets. Spread all of the pistachio over the phyllo. Cover with the rest of the phyllo sheets. With very sharp knife, cut diagonally across the pan to make small diamonds. And brush with melted butter, use all the melted butter. Bake until evenly browned and crispy about 1-1/2 hours. Meanwhile, prepare syrup and set aside to cool.

Sugar Syrup: Over medium heat combine all ingredients, bring to boil, stirring to dissolve sugar. Reduce heat and simmer 10 minutes. Strain and cool to room temperature.

Remove pastry from oven, cool slightly, and pour cooled syrup evenly over the top; it should penetrate all of the layers. Cool several hours. If you are using walnuts you can grind them with 2 teaspoons of cinnamon. Serves 36.

## Tel Kadayif

*-Turkish-*
*1 pounds shredded dough*
  *Turkish tel kadayifi*
*3 sticks (4-ounce each) unsalted*
  *butter or margarine, melted*
*3 cups chopped walnut*
*1 teaspoon cinnamon*

*Sugar syrup:*
*5 cups water*
*2-1/2 cups sugar*
*2 teaspoons lemon juice*

Tel kadayif is a confection made from a shredded phyllo-type dough, which is drenched in syrup and filled and sprinkled with chopped walnuts. Tel kadayifi can be found in some Middle Eastern grocery stores. There are several ways to prepare desserts with tel kadayifi, here is one of them:

Melt 1/4 of the butter or margarine. Grease large baking pan with the melted butter. Lay down half the tel kadayifi. Meanwhile prepare filling. Mix chopped walnut with 1 teaspoon cinnamon. Sprinkle walnut-cinnamon filling over tel kadayifi. Cover filling with the rest of the kadayif. Sprinkle remaining butter over the kadayif evenly. Bake at 375 °F until top is golden, about 20-25 minutes. Remove from oven.

Sugar syrup: Over medium-high heat, combine water, sugar and lemon juice to make syrup. Bring to boil; stirring to dissolve the sugar. Reduce heat, simmer 10 minutes. Remove from heat. Ladle hot syrup over warm tel kadayifi. Cool before serving, garnish with chopped walnuts. Cut into squares. Serves 8-10.

## Chocolate Sack

*-French-*
*1 sheet frozen puff pastry*
*1 package (8-oz.) semisweet*
  *chocolate bits*
*1/3 cup chopped walnuts*

*2 tablespoons unsalted butter*
  *or margarine*
*1 tablespoon Grand Marnier (optional)*
*Confectioners' sugar*

Thaw pastry 20 minutes. Preheat oven to 425 °F. On a lightly floured board, roll pastry to a 14-inch square. In the center of the square, place chocolate, walnuts and butter; sprinkle with Grand Marnier. Pull pastry edges together, twist and turn. Place on ungreased baking sheet and bake for 20 minutes. Let stand at least 10 minutes. Sprinkle with confectioners' sugar and serve. Serves 6.

# Kazandibi

-Turkish-
1-quart milk
1 cup sugar
5 tablespoons rice flour
5 tablespoons corn starch
1-1/4 cups water
1/2 to 1 teaspoon vanilla extract
6 to 8 tablespoons confectioner's sugar
Ground cinnamon

This is one of most popular of the healthy milk-based traditional Turkish desserts. You can find it in many dessert shops in Turkey.

In large saucepan, over medium-high heat, heat milk and sugar to boil; stirring until sugar dissolves. Remove from heat. Meanwhile in small bowl filled with 1-1/4 cups water, mix rice flour and corn starch and add to the milk mixture. Place saucepan over heat. Over medium-low heat cook, until mixture becomes thicker, stirring constantly, do not boil at any time (about 60 minutes). When it is done it should be thicker than rice pudding. Add vanilla extract; stir it. Remove from heat; stir constantly while cooling it. In 24x30-inch baking pan, sprinkle half of the confectioners' sugar. Place baking pan into oven and burn the sugar slightly. Add rest of the confectioners' sugar. Pour thick milk mixture over the sugar. In preheated oven at 350 °F; bake until bottom of milk mixture browns. Remove pan from oven. Immediately, place the bottom of the hot pan into cold water in order to remove the kazandibi easily. Cool it; cut into rectangles; roll the kazandibi pieces brown sides out. Sprinkle with cinnamon. Serve cold. Serves 6.

# Banana Soufflé

-French-
3 large bananas
1 tablespoon lemon juice
1/3 cup sugar
1 tablespoon cornstarch
1/2 teaspoon ground nutmeg
1/4 teaspoon grated lemon peel
1/8 teaspoon salt
3/4 cup milk
3 large eggs, separated
2 tablespoons unsalted butter
    or margarine, melted
1-1/2 teaspoons vanilla extract
1 cup heavy or whipping cream,
    whipped

Grease bottom of 1-1/2 quart souffle dish. Peel and slice bananas. In covered blender container at medium speed, blend bananas and lemon juice until well mixed and creamy.

In 3-quart saucepan, mix sugar, cornstarch, nutmeg, lemon peel and salt. Stir in milk until blended. Over medium heat, cook milk mixture until thickened, stirring constantly. Remove from heat.

Preheat oven to 375 °F. In small bowl with fork, beat egg yolks well. Add a little of hot-milk mixture; mix together well. Mix egg-yolk mixture well with remaining hot-milk mixture. Stir in butter or margarine, vanilla extract and banana mixture. In small bowl with mixer at high speed, beat egg whites until stiff peaks form. Carefully fold into banana mixture and pour into soufflé dish. Bake 35 minutes or until golden brown. Serve immediately with whipped cream to spoon over the top. Serves 8.

# Chocolate Mousse with Raspberries

8 ounces semisweet chocolate
3 tablespoons powdered sugar
3 tablespoons brewed coffee

2-3 egg yolks
1-1/4 cups whipping cream
1/2 cup raspberries

Melt chocolate in double-boiler or in pan with hot water. Add sugar, coffee and egg yolks, one at a time, Stir until mixture has thickened. Remove from heat; let cool. Whip cream. Add to slightly cooled chocolate mixture. Spoon mousse into individual serving dishes. Cover.

Let cool in refrigerator for 1 hour. Garnish each serving with a spoonful of whipped cream and raspberries. Serve with dessert wine. Serves 4.


# Crêpes Suzette

*-French-*
*Crêpes:*
**Unsalted butter, melted**
**1-1/2 cups milk**
**2/3 cups all-purpose flour**
**1/2 teaspoon salt**
**3 eggs**
**1/4 cup orange flavor liqueur**

*Suzette Sauce:*
**1/3 cup orange juice**
**1/4 cup butter**
**2 tablespoons sugar**
**1/4 teaspoon grated orange peel**

In medium bowl with wire whisk, beat 2 tablespoons butter and remaining crêpe ingredients until smooth. Cover; chill 2 hours. Brush bottom of 7-inch crêpe-pan and 10-inch skillet with melted butter. Over medium heat, heat pans; pour scant 1/4 cup batter into crêpe pan, tip pan to coat bottom; cook 2 minutes till top is set, underside slightly browned. Loosen crêpe; invert into hot 10-inch skillet; cook other side 30 seconds. Slip crêpe onto waxed paper. Meanwhile, start cooking another crêpe. Stack crêpes between waxed paper. Use immediately or wrap in foil and refrigerate. About 30 minutes before serving. Prepare suzette sauce. Fold crêpes in quarters; arrange in Suzette sauce. Simmer over medium-low heat 10 minutes; pour liqueur in center (do not stir). Heat liqueur one minute or two; light with along match and flame. Or, in 1-quart saucepan over low heat, heat liqueur just until warm. Carefully light warm liqueur with long match and pour over crêpes in chafing dish. Serve the crêpes immediately.

Suzette Sauce: In chafing dish or 10-inch skillet over low heat, heat 1/3 cup orange juice, 1/4 cup butter, 2 tablespoons sugar and 1/4 teaspoon grated orange peel until butter melts. Serves 6.

## Pineapple Rings

3 cups bread flour
1 package active dry yeast
  or quick rise yeast
1/4 cup sugar
1-1/2 teaspoons salt
1/4 cup oil
2 eggs
1/3 cup milk
1/3 cup water

Filling:
1/4 cup unsalted butter or margarine
1 cup powdered sugar
1/2 cup finely chopped pecans
1/2 cup candied pineapple,
  finely chopped
Glaze:
1/4 cup pineapple juice
3 tablespoons sugar

In large mixer bowl, combine 2 cups bread flour, yeast, sugar and salt; mix well. Heat milk, water and 1/4 cup oil until very warm. Add to flour mixture; add eggs. Blend at low speed until moistened; beat 3 minutes at medium speed. By hand, gradually stir in enough remaining flour to make a soft dough. Cover; let rise in warm place about 30 minutes. (15 minutes for quick rise yeast).

Prepare filling: Cream 1/4 cup butter; blend in powdered sugar. Stir in pecans and pineapple.

On lightly floured surface, roll dough to a 12x12-inch square. Spread filling over half dough. Fold uncovered dough over filling. Cut into 12 strips. Twist strips twice; loosely coil on greased cookie sheet, tucking ends under. Cover; let rise in warm place about 50 minutes (30 minutes for quick rise yeast). Bake at 375 °F for 15 minutes.

Prepare Glaze: Combine pineapple juice and sugar; brush rolls; bake 5 to 7 minutes longer until golden brown. Remove from cookie sheets; cool. Serves 6-8.

## Strawberry-Raisin Scone

-Italian-
2 cups all-purpose flour
2 tablespoons sugar
2 tablespoons baking powder
1/4 teaspoon salt
1/2 cup unsalted butter

1/2 cup milk
2 eggs, beaten
3/4 cup seedless raisins
1/2 cup thick strawberry jam

Heat oven to 425 °F. Grease 8-inch round cake pan. Combine flour, sugar, baking powder and salt. Using pastry blender or fork, cut in butter until mixture resembles coarse crumbs. Add milk, eggs and raisins; stir just until dry ingredients are moistened. With floured hands, pat half of dough into bottom of greased pan; press dough 1/4-inch up sides. Spread jam on dough. Top with remaining dough; spread evenly. Using sharp knife, score dough into 8 wedges. Brush top lightly with melted butter and sprinkle with sugar, if desired. Bake at 425 °F for 20 to 25 minutes or until wooden pick inserted in center comes out clean. Serve warm. Serves 8.

## Caramel Walnut Bars

*Crust:*
*2 cups all-purpose flour*
*2 cups firmly packed*
  *brown sugar*
*1/2 cup unsalted butter, softened*
*1 cup pecan halves*

*Filling:*
*2/3 cup unsalted butter*
*1/2 cup firmly packed brown sugar*
*1/2 cup butterscotch flavored chips*
*1/2 cup semisweet chocolate chips*

Preheat oven to 350 °F. In large mixer bowl combine all crust ingredients except pecans. Beat at medium speed, scraping bowl often, until well mixed and particles are fine (2 to 3 minutes). Press on bottom of 13x9-inch baking pan. Sprinkle pecans evenly over unbaked crust. In 1-quart saucepan, combine 2/3 cup butter and 1/2 cup brown sugar. Cook over medium heat, stirring constantly, until mixture comes to a full boil (4 to 5 minutes). Boil, stirring constantly, until slightly thickened. Pour over pecans and crust. Bake for 18 to 20 minutes or until entire caramel layer is bubbly. Immediately sprinkle with butter scotch and chocolate chips. Allow to melt slightly (3 to 5 minutes). Swirl chips leaving some whole for a marbled effect. Cool completely; cut into bars. Makes 5 dozen.

## Raisin Cookies

*2-1/4 cups all-purpose flour*
*1-1/2 cups sugar*
*1 cup butter or margarine,*
  *softened*
*3 eggs,*
*1 teaspoon double-acting*
  *baking powder*

*1 teaspoon salt*
*1 teaspoon vanilla extract*
*1-1/2 cups seedless raisins*
*2 tablespoons grated orange peel*

Preheat oven to 375 °F. Grease 2 large cookie sheets. Into large bowl, measure all ingredients except raisins and orange peel. With mixer at low speed, beat ingredients until just mixed. Increase speed to medium and beat 2 minutes, occasionally scraping bowl with rubber spatula. Stir in raisins and orange peel. Drop batter by heaping tablespoonfuls, about 2 inches apart, on cookie sheets. Bake 15 minutes or until cookies are golden brown. Remove cookies to wire racks to cool. Makes 30 cookies.

# Chocolate Chip Cookies

1 (9 oz.) milk chocolate bar
1 cup unsalted butter, softened
1/3 cup granulated sugar
1/3 cup packed light brown
  sugar

1 teaspoon vanilla extract
2 cups all-purpose flour
1 cups mini morsel chocolate chips

Heat oven to 375 °F. Divide chocolate bar into 1-inch small pieces. In large mixing bowl, beat butter, granulated sugar, brown sugar and vanilla until well blended. Add flour; blend until smooth. Stir in small chocolate chips. Mold scant tablespoon dough around each chocolate piece, covering completely. Shape into balls; place on ungreased cookie sheet. Bake 10 to 12 minutes or until set. Cool slightly; remove from cookie sheet to wire rack. Cool completely. Makes 4 dozen.

# Cafe Vienna's Pistachio Christmas Ribbons

-Austrian-
Cookie layer:
3/4 cup unsalted butter
1/2 cup sugar
2 cups all-purpose flour
1 teaspoon baking powder
1/4 teaspoon salt
2 tablespoons lemon juice
1 cup raspberry jam

Pistachio Marzipan Layer:
1 cup raw (unroasted) pistachios
1/4 cup butter or margarine, softened
1/2 cup sugar
2 eggs
1 tablespoon grated lemon peel

Prepare cookie layer: Preheat oven to 350 °F. Grease 9-inch square baking pan. In large bowl, with electric mixer at medium speed, beat butter with sugar until creamy. Add flour, baking powder, salt and lemon juice; beat until mixture forms a soft dough. Press dough lightly into prepared pan. Bake 20 minutes or just until edges begin to turn golden.

Meanwhile Prepare Pistachio Marzipan Layer: In food processor, combine pistachios, butter, sugar, eggs and lemon peel; process until blended to a paste (or grind pistachios in blender; beat in remaining ingredients using an electric mixer).

To assemble, spread jam evenly over warm, baked cookie layer. Refrigerate 20 minutes or until set. Carefully spread an even layer of marzipan over jam. Return to oven and bake 30 minutes longer or until edges begin to turn light brown. Cool completely in pan on wire rack. To serve, cut into 2-1/4-by 1-inch bars. Place each bar on its side in small ruffled candy cup if desired. Makes 3 dozen bars.

## Mint Flavored Chocolate Cookies

*-American-*

*1-1/2 cups all-purpose flour*
*1-1/2 teaspoons baking powder*
*1/4 teaspoon salt*
*1 (10-ounce) mint flavored*
  *semisweet chocolate mini*
  *morsels*

*6 tablespoons unsalted butter, softened*
*1 cup sugar*
*1-1/2 teaspoons vanilla extract*
*2 eggs*
*Confectioners' sugar*

In bowl, combine flour, baking powder and salt; set aside. Over hot (not boiling) water, melt 1 cup mini morsels; stirring until smooth. In bowl, beat butter and sugar until creamy. Add melted mint morsels and vanilla. Beat in eggs. Gradually beat in flour mixture. Stir in remaining 1/2 cup mint morsels. Wrap dough in plastic wrap; freeze until firm. Preheat oven to 350 °F. Shape dough into 1-inch balls; coat with confectioners' sugar. Place on ungreased cookie sheet. Bake 10-12 minutes, until tops appear cracked. Let stand 5 minutes on cookie sheet. Cool completely. Makes 30 cookies.


## Peanut Butter Fudge Filled Cookies

*-American-*

*Cookies:*
*3 cups all-purpose flour*
*1-1/4 cups unsalted butter or*
  *margarine, softened*
*1/2 cup granulated sugar*
*1 tablespoon vanilla extract*
*Powdered sugar*

*Filling:*
*1 package (8 ounces) semisweet*
  *chocolate baking bars*
*1/3 cup peanut butter*
*1/4 cup sifted powdered sugar*
*Candy corn (optional)*

For cookies: In large bowl, combine flour, butter, sugar and vanilla; knead until well blended. Measure dough by tablespoon; roll into balls. Place on ungreased baking sheets. Make deep wells in centers with thumb. Bake in preheated 400 °F oven for 8 to 10 minutes or until set. Press centers of cookies down slightly. Cool completely; dust with powdered sugar.

For filling: In small, heavy saucepan over low heat, melt baking bars and peanut butter, stirring until smooth. Cool slightly. Stir in powdered sugar. Drop by rounded teaspoonfuls into center of each cookie. Decorate with candy corn. Makes 3 dozen cookies.

## Harrod's Rich Chocolate-Walnut Clusters

5 squares unsweetened
  chocolate, melted
1/4 cup cocoa powder
1/2 cup all-purpose flour
1/2 cup sugar

1/4 cup unsalted butter
  or margarine, softened
1 egg
1/2 teaspoon salt
1-1/2 teaspoons vanilla extract
2 cups chopped walnuts

Preheat oven to 350 °F. Grease cookie sheets. In large bowl with mixer at medium speed, beat all ingredients except walnuts until well mixed, occasionally scraping bowl with rubber spatula. Stir in walnuts.

Drop mixture by rounded teaspoonfuls, 1/2-inch apart, onto cookie sheets. Bake 10 minutes. Remove cookies to wire racks; cool. Makes 30 cookies.

## Amaretto Bars

1-1/2 cups all-purpose flour
1/2 cup confectioners' sugar
3/4 cup cold unsalted butter
  or margarine
1 tablespoon cornstarch
3 to 4 tablespoons Amaretto
  liqueur
1 can (14-ounces) sweetened
  condensed milk

1 package (6 ounces) semisweet
  chocolate chips
1 can (3-1/2 ounces) flaked coconut
  (1-1/3 cups)
1/2 cup sliced almonds

Preheat oven to 350 °F. Grease 13x9-inch baking pan. In large bowl, combine flour and sugar. With pastry blender or two knives, cut in butter until crumbly. Press mixture firmly on bottom of prepared pan. Bake 20 minutes. Meanwhile, in small bowl, stir cornstarch into Amaretto; stir in sweetened condensed milk. Pour mixture evenly over prepared crust. Top with the chocolate chips, coconut and almonds; press down firmly. Bake 25 to 30 minutes, or until golden brown. Cool in pan on wire rack. Refrigerate until ready to serve. To serve, cut into bars. Makes 2 dozen bars.

## Raspberry Coconut Layer Bars

*-Swiss-*

1-2/3 cups Graham cracker crumbs
1/2 cup unsalted butter or
  margarine, melted
2-2/3 cups (7-ounce) package
  flaked coconut
1-1/4 cups (14-ounce can)
  sweetened, condensed milk
1 cup red raspberry jam or
  preserves

1/3 cup finely chopped walnuts,
  toasted
1/2 cup semisweet chocolate morsels,
  melted
1/4 cup (1-1/2 ounces) melted white
  chocolate baking bar
1/4 cup melted dark chocolate bar

In medium bowl, combine cracker crumbs and melted butter. Spread evenly over bottom of 13x9-inch baking pan, pressing to make compact crust. Sprinkle coconut over crust. Pour sweetened condensed milk evenly over coconut. Bake in preheated 350 °F oven for 20 to 25 minutes or until lightly browned; cool. Spread jam over coconut layer; chill 3 to 4 hours. Sprinkle with walnuts. Drizzle dark chocolate then white chocolate over top layer to make lacy effect; chill. Cut into 3x1-1/2-inch bars. Makes 24 bar cookies.


## Austrian Linzer Cookies

*-Austrian-*

1 (3-1/2 to 4-ounce) can blanched
  silvered almonds, ground
1 egg
2 cups all-purpose flour
1 cup sugar
3/4 cup unsalted butter,
  softened

1 teaspoon cinnamon
1 teaspoon grated lemon peel
1/8 teaspoon ground cloves
1/2 (12-ounce) jar apricot
  jam

In large bowl with mixer at low speed, beat all ingredients except jam until well mixed, occasionally scraping bowl (mixture will be crumbly). Shape dough into ball; wrap; chill until easy to handle, about 2 hours.

Preheat oven to 350 °F. Grease 11x7-inch baking pan. Press half of dough into pan (keep remaining chilled). Spread jam over dough in pan. Roll half of remaining dough into six 11-inch long ropes; arrange lengthwise, one inch apart on jam. Roll remaining dough into eight 7-inch long ropes; arrange crosswise over jam. Bake 40 minutes or until top is golden. Cool in pan on wire rack. Cut into 2x1-inch bars. Makes 30 bars.

# Espresso-Pistachio Cookie Balls

3/4 cup (1-1/2 sticks) unsalted
butter or margarine
1/2 cup granulated sugar
2 cups all-purpose flour
2-1/2 tablespoons instant
espresso coffee granules
1 egg

2 squares (2-ounces) semisweet
chocolate, melted and cooled
3/4 cup finely chopped pistachios
Confectioners' sugar
Chocolate topping

Chocolate Topping:
2 squares (2-ounces)
semisweet chocolate
1 tablespoon confectioner'
sugar

Preheat oven to 350 °F. In large bowl with electric mixer at medium speed, beat butter and granulated sugar until blended. Add flour, espresso granules, egg and melted chocolate, beating until smooth. Stir in pistachios. Shape dough into 1-inch balls; place on ungreased cookie sheet. Bake 8 minutes or until firm; cookies should feel dry to the touch. Transfer cookies to wire racks; cool 15 minutes. Sprinkle partially cooled cookies with confectioners' sugar or chocolate topping; cool completely.

(Note: To prepare dough in food processor, combine butter, sugar, flour, espresso granules, egg and melted chocolate in work bowl. Pulse on and off until ingredients are blended to a smooth dough, scraping down dough once with rubber spatula. Scrape sides of processor down; add chopped pistachios. Push on and off to mix).

Chocolate Topping: In food processor, process chocolate until finely ground. Add sugar; process to mix. Place mixture in sieve and tap lightly over cooling cookies.

# Coconut Meringues

2 egg whites
1/8 teaspoon cream of tartar
3/4 cup confectioners' sugar

1/4 cup shredded coconut
1/4 teaspoon almond extract

Preheat oven to 250 °F. In small bowl with mixer at high speed, beat egg whites and cream of tartar until soft peaks form. Beating at high speed, gradually sprinkle in sugar, 2 tablespoons at a time, beating until sugar is completely dissolved (whites should stand in stiff glossy peaks). With rubber spatula, fold in coconut and extract until mixed.

Drop mixture by rounded teaspoonfuls onto large cookie sheet, about 1-inch apart. Bake 1 hour or until dry. Remove to rack to cool. Makes 2 dozen cookies.

## Almond Cookies-Aci Badem Kurabiyesi

*-Turkish-*

*1 roll (7-ounce) almond paste*
*3/4 cup granulated sugar*
*1/4 cup finely ground almonds*

*2 egg whites, slightly beaten*
*1 tablespoon flour*
*Whole almonds for topping*

Blend almond paste and sugar in electric mixer. Add egg whites until smooth but not runny, add flour, mix well, finally add ground almond and mix it. Pipe out on greased and floured aluminum foil to a diameter of 1-1/2-inch. Leave room for kurabiyes to double in size. Bake at 325 °F for 15 minutes or until golden. Do not remove from aluminium foil until cool. Before baking, you can top each round of dough with one whole almond (optional). Makes 15 cookies.


## Italian Biscotti di Mandorle

*-Italian-*

*1 cup finely chopped walnuts*
*2 teaspoons anise seeds*
*1 cup sugar*
*1/2 cup (1 stick) butter, softened*
*2 teaspoons vanilla extract*
*1/2 teaspoon salt*
*1/4 teaspoon grated orange peel*
*3 eggs*

*2-1/2 cups all-purpose flour*
*1-1/2 teaspoons baking powder*
*1/4 cup chopped red candied cherries*
*1/4 cup chopped green candied cherries*
*Chocolate Glaze:*
*1 package (12 ounces) semisweet*
  *chocolate chips*
*1/2 cup (1 stick) cold butter*

Preheat oven to 325 °F. In medium-sized skillet, combine walnuts and anise seeds. Place over low heat and cook about 5 minutes or until golden, stirring constantly. Remove from skillet; place in medium-sized bowl to cool. In large bowl with electric mixer at medium speed, beat sugar, butter, vanilla, salt and orange peel until light and fluffy. Beat in eggs, one at a time until well combined. In medium-sized bowl, combine flour and baking powder; stir in reserved nut mixture. Gradually add to butter mixture, mixing until combined. Stir in candied red and green cherries.

Divide dough in half. On ungreased cookie sheet, shape each half into a log about 1-1/2 inches in diameter; place logs 2 to 3 inches apart. Bake about 25 minutes or until well browned. Reduce oven temperature to 250 °F. Cut logs diagonally into 1/2-inch thick slices; arrange slices cut sides down, on two cookie sheets. Bake about 10 minutes longer or until dried. Remove cookies to wire racks to cool completely. Meanwhile, prepare chocolate glaze. Dip cooled cookies halfway into chocolate glaze. Place on wire racks; let stand about 1 hour or until glaze is set. Store in layers separated by waxed paper in airtight container.

Chocolate Glaze: In small saucepan over very low heat, heat chocolate and butter until melted, stirring occasionally. Makes 16 biscotti.

# Chewy Raisin Walnut Shortbread Bars

1-1/4 cups all-purpose flour
1/2 cups sugar
1/2 cup butter or margarine
2 eggs
1/2 cup firmly packed
  brown sugar

1 teaspoon vanilla
1/3 teaspoon baking soda
1 cup chopped walnuts
1 cup seedless raisins
1/2 cup flaked coconut

Preheat oven to 350 °F. Lightly grease 8-inch square pan. Combine flour and sugar. Using pastry blender or fork, cut in butter until mixture resembles fine meal. Press into greased pan. Bake for 20 minutes or just until edges are lightly golden. Meanwhile, combine eggs, brown sugar and vanilla; beat well. Stir in baking soda, walnuts, raisins and coconut. Spoon over hot crust; spread to cover evenly. Return to oven; bake an additional 20 to 25 minutes or until top is set. Cool completely. Cut into bars. Makes 20 bars.

# Baked Quince-Firinda Ayva Tatlisi

-Turkish-
2 medium size quinces
1 cup Turkish quince preserve
2 cups sugar

4 cups water
1 teaspoon vanilla extract
Vanilla ice cream

The quince is a yellow colored and slightly sour fruit, commonly found in The Mediterranean region. To avoid loosing the juice, most of the time it is eaten with spoon.

Baked quince: Cut quinces in half, remove seeds from the center. Meanwhile mix sugar, vanilla and water. Heat until syrup boils; add quince; cook until quinces are soft. Remove from heat, reserve syrup; top the quince halves with quince preserve. Place them in jelly-roll pan. Ladle half of the syrup over quince. Bake at 400 °F until tops are slightly golden. Ladle remaining syrup over quince. Serve warm, if you like with vanilla ice cream. This dessert traditionally served with "Kaymak". Kaymak is popular in Turkey and The Balkans and is made from milk. Clotted cream and creme fraîche are similar, except that creme fraîche is not as rich or thick. Kaymak, nearly as thick as butter, is served to accompany traditional desserts and baked fruits. True kaymak is for those who really appreciate the work involved in making it and revere such culinary treasures. Serves 4.

## Soft Chestnut Candies-Çikolatali Kestane Sekeri

*-Turkish-*

*1 (18-oz.) can Turkish candied chestnuts in heavy syrup*
*1/4 pound semisweet chocolate*

*1/2 cup milk*
*1/2 cup whole unsalted raw pistachios, ground coarsely*

Turkish candied chestnuts in heavy syrup can be found in Turkish grocery stores. Reserve 3 to 4 chestnuts in small cup; set aside. In medium bowl, place rest of the sweet chestnut candy and 1/4 of the sweet syrup, mash with a fork, stir in coarsely ground pistachios. Lay out a sheet of aluminum foil, shape mashed mixture into balls while placing large chestnut pieces into center of each ball. Meanwhile in small saucepan, melt chocolate with milk. If you need, add more milk. Make a heavy chocolate sauce, dip chestnut-pistachio balls in this chocolate sauce, place them on the foil, chill; keep in refrigerator until serving time. Makes 10 to 15 candies.

## Grapefruit Ambrosia

*1-16-ounce can grapefruit sections*

*1/4 cup honey*
*1/2 cup flaked coconut*

Thoroughly drain liquid from grapefruit sections; set aside for use another day. In bowl, toss well, grapefruit sections, honey and coconut. Serve immediately. Serves 4.

## Pineapple Fruit Bowl

*1 whole large pineapple*
*Sliced melon pieces*
*Oranges, peeled*
*Nectarines, sliced, unpeeled*

*Plums, sliced*
*Grapes*
*Strawberries*
*1/4 cup Scotch whiskey (optional)*

Cut pineapple lengthwise, Remove pulp and cut pulp into triangles. Mix gently all sliced fruits and pineapple pieces with grapes, pour 1/4 cup Scotch whiskey (optional) over the mixture. Place fruits in pineapple bowls. Serves 8.

# Vanilla Ice Cream with Brandied Morello-Cherry Sauce

*-Turkish-*
*1 cup Turkish Morello*
*cherry preserves*
*1/2 cup brandy*

*1/2 teaspoon cornstarch*
*1/4 teaspoon almond extract*
*Vanilla ice cream*

You can find Turkish Morello cherry preserves in Middle Eastern grocery stores. Turkish Morello cherry preserves are made from Mediterranean Morello cherries and they have nicely balanced sweet-sour taste. In 2-quart saucepan combine first 3 ingredients. Over medium heat, cook, stirring constantly, until mixture is thickened and boils; remove from heat. Stir in almond extract. Serve warm or cover and refrigerate, serve over vanilla ice cream. Serves 4.

# Tutto's Pistachio Covered Ice Cream with Fresh Fruits

*1 cup finely ground pistachios*
*1 (6 oz.) bar white chocolate*
*1/2 cup milk*
*1/2 cup strawberry jelly*

*2 teaspoons brandy*
*Sliced kiwis, whole*
*red raspberries*
*Vanilla ice cream*

In small saucepan, over low heat, melt white chocolate with milk to make white chocolate sauce, set aside, in small saucepan heat strawberry preserve with brandy to make strawberry-brandy sauce, stir to mix. Keep them warm. Scoop vanilla ice cream on serving plate, top with ground pistachios, decorate plate with white chocolate sauce, strawberry-brandy sauce, sliced kiwis and red raspberries. Serve with dessert wine.

# DRINKS

# Irish coffee

*-Irish-*
*1-1/2 teaspoons sugar*
*1 jigger Irish whiskey*

*Hot strong black coffee*
*Whipped cream*

Into 6- or 8-ounce stemmed glass or coffee cup, measure sugar and Irish whisky. Add hot coffee to fill glass to within 1/2-inch of top; stir to dissolve sugar completely. Top with a spoonful of whipped cream; do not stir. Sip coffee through cream. Serves to: 1

# Munich Nights

*2 teaspoons dried orange peel*
*1 teaspoon whole cloves*
*4 whole cardamom, cracked*
*3 short cinnamon sticks*
*Cheesecloth*
*1 cup dark seedless raisins*
*1 (8-ounce) package dried*
*  apricots*

*6-1/2 cups Burgundy*
*3 1/4 cups vodka or gin*
*3/4 cup sugar*
*1 cup whole blanched almonds*

Place orange peel and spices on a piece of cheesecloth; tie with string to form a bag. In covered, 4-quart saucepan over medium-low heat, simmer raisins, apricots, spice bag and half of the burgundy 30 minutes. Remove from heat and discard spice bag; stir in vodka, sugar and remaining Burgundy; cover mixture and let stand overnight at room temperature. To serve: Over high heat, heat mixture until piping hot, but not boiling, stirring occasionally. Ignite mixture with long match; let burn a few seconds, then cover pan to extinguish flame. Add almonds; pour into heated punch bowl. Serve hot. Serves 20.

# Hot Mulled Wine

*-German-*
*4 cups sugar*
*1 tablespoon ground cinnamon*
*  or 6 cinnamon sticks*
*1 teaspoon ground cloves or*
*  whole cloves*

*2 cups boiling water*
*3 medium oranges, thinly sliced*
*1 medium lemon, thinly sliced*
*1 gallon dry red wine*

In 8-quart saucepot, combine sugar, cinnamon, cloves and water. Add orange and lemon slices to saucepot. Over high heat, heat to boiling; boil 5 minutes, stirring occasionally. Reduce heat to medium; add wine; heat till piping hot but bot boiling. Stirring occasionally. Carefully ladle individual servings of hot into punch cups or heat-safe glasses. Serves 20.

## Bora Bora

1/2 oz. rum
1/2 oz. peach schnapps
1/2 oz. vodka
Ice cubes

3 oz. orange juice
Orange, grapefruit slices and
     strawberries

Combine all ingredients, stir it well, serve over ice; decorate with orange, grapefruit slices and strawberries.

## Cozumel

1/2 cup lemon juice
1/2 cup orange juice
1/2 cup sugar
3-1/4 cups dry red wine
1/4 cup brandy

1 (7-ounce) bottle club soda, chilled
1 cup fruit (sliced orange, lemon,
     apple, peach, banana)
1 tray ice cubes

Into large pitcher, pour lemon juice, orange juice and sugar; stir to dissolve sugar. Stir in remaining ingredients. To serve, pour into glasses making sure each person gets some fruit.

## Turkish Coffee

1/4 cup water
1 teaspoon Turkish coffee

Tools for preparing:
Turkish coffee pot "Cezve"
Fincan (small espresso cup)
     for serving

Volumes have been written about Turkish coffee; its history, significance in social life, and the ambiance of coffee houses. Without some understanding of this background, it is easy to be disappointed by the tiny brew with the annoying grounds on which an uninitiated traveler like Mark Twain may accidently end up chewing. A few words of caution will have to suffice for the purposes of this brief primer. First, grounds are not to be swallowed; so, sip the coffee gingerly. Secondly, do not expect a caffeine surge with one shot of Turkish coffee, it is not "strong", just thick. Third, remember that it is the setting and the company that matters; the coffee is just an excuse for the occasion.

Combine water, coffee, sugar to taste in small cup with a handle on the side (Turkish coffee pot-"Cezve"), over medium-low heat, heat (Do not boil), stirring. Slowly pour coffee into "Fincan" (Espresso cup). You can find small Turkish coffee pots and cups in Middle Eastern grocery stores. Serves 1.

# HERBS

### Allspice
Whole or ground berries with a flavor resembling a blend of cloves, cinnamon and nutmeg. Used in baking, some meat and vegetable dishes, pickles, and relishes.

### Aniseed
The small brown seed of anise plant, with a sweet, potent licorice taste.

### Basil
Distinct with its broad emerald-green leaves and vibrant anise-like flavor, basil comes in several varieties, including green, purple and lemon. Used mostly in Italian dishes.

### Bay Leaves
Fresh or dried leaves used in meat, poultry and fish dishes; their strong flavor mellows during long cooking. Remove the leaves before serving. Popular in Turkish cuisine.

### Caraway seed
Whole seeds with a warm and slightly sharp taste. Related to anise, they are used in breads, cheese spreads and dips.

### Cardamom
This greenish-tan coffee-bean-size pod has a lingering perfume and sweet warmish taste. Cardamom is sold in three forms; whole pods; hard black seeds found inside the pods; and powdered. It is often used in Turkish cuisine for breads and pastries.

### Chive
Chives have the softest flavor of any member of the onion family. Purple chive flower buds are delectable in salads.

### Cilantro
Also known as Chinese parsley, this pungent aromatic herb is the leafy part of the coriander plant.

### Cinnamon stick
Most spices are seed pods, but cinnamon is the bark of a tropical evergreen tree that bears its name. Powdered cinnamon is often used in Turkish desserts and hot drinks.

### Coriander
Coriander is the small, round and ridged highly aromatic seed of the coriander plant, whose leaves from the herb cilantro.

### Cumin

This small brown sickle-shaped seed has a pungent, earthy and musky aroma.

### Curry powder

Curry is a blend of a dozen or more spices. Although the precise formula varies, the main ingredients in curry powder include turmeric, coriander, cumin, cayenne, cardamom, cinnamon and ginger.

### Dill Weed

Often this fragrant herb with thin feathery leaves is used in Europe and Mediterranean (especially in Turkey) to flavor soups, vegetable and fish dishes.

### Ginger

Whole root used crystallized (candied), fresh, preserved in syrup, or dried and ground. Used in Oriental-style meat, poultry, seafood and vegetable dishes, and with fruit.

### Marjoram

Bittersweet fresh or dried leaves used in meat, poultry and Italian-style dishes.

### Mint

Leaves with a sweet aroma and cool aftertaste. Used fresh or dried with vegetables, fruits and desserts and sauces.

### Nutmeg

Native to Indonesia, nutmeg is a finely veined oval nut with a musky cinnamon-and-vanilla aroma.

### Oregano

A member of the mint family, this fragrant plant has small oval pungent-tasting leaves. Oregano is equally at home in Italian, Cuban and Mexican cooking.

### Paprika

Ground pods of sweet chilies or peppers, hot to mild and sweet in flavor. Mostly used in meat, poultry and cheese dishes.

### Parsley

This popular garnish comes in two forms: flat-leaf (also called Turkish or Italian parsley) and curly leaf. Choose flat-leaf parsley over its curly counterpart for a more vibrant flavor.

### Poppy seed

Poppy seeds are crunchy with a sweet, mild, nutty flavor. Used whole in breads, pastries and cakes.

### Rosemary

A member of the evergreen family, rosemary has slender firm leaves that are dark-green on one side and silver-green on the other. Rosemary pairs nicely with lamb and chicken dishes with its sharp pine-like taste.

### Saffron

Saffron is the fragrant rusty-red stigmas of a crocus flower grown in southern Spain. To make a single pound of saffron, 70,000 flowers must be picked and processed by hand.

### Sage

Fresh or dried aromatic leaves. Used in liver, pork, poultry and cheese dishes.

### Savory

Winter savory and summer savory are the most common varieties. Used fresh or dried in meat, egg and rice dishes.

### Sesame seed

Sesame seeds are flat with a nut like flavor; they are mostly used in Chinese-style dishes, Turkish and Chinese style breads, snacks and candy.

### Tarragon

Associated with European and Turkish cooking, tarragon has bright-green spear-shaped leaves with an elegant anise flavor. It is used mostly used in salads, meat and fish dishes, and with their accompanying sauces.

### Thyme

Thyme has been used as an antiseptic since ancient times. It is mostly used in meat and fish dishes, and comes in numerous varieties including lemon, orange and mint.

### Turmeric

Closely related to ginger, this mild-tasting spice turns curry powder and ballpark-style mustard golden-yellow.

### Vanilla

Vanilla is the rich, sweet seedpod of an orchid native to central America.

### Wasabi

Often called Japanese horseradish, wasabi is the fiery-flavored root of the mountain hollyhock.

**FAVORITES
From The
WORLD'S
BEST CUISINES**

*A World of Great Taste!*

Ela Kozak Küçükçakar

*Favorites from
the World's
Best Cuisines is
available for gifts!*

*Share Ela's delicious
recipes with your
friends!*

## MAIL TO:

Ela Küçükçakar
P.O. Box 25152
Tempe, Arizona 85285

**Send Money Order, Personal Or Cashiers Check
(U.S. Funds Only) Payable To: Ela Küçükçakar**

- - - - - ✂ - - - - - - - - - - - - - - - - - - - - - - - - - - - - - - - - - - - - - - - - - - - - ✂ - - - - - - - -

(Please Print Only)

_____BOOKS ORDERED

X $24.95 EACH=_____
(Sales Tax Included)

DATE_____/_____/_____

S/H $4.00 PER ORDER _____

*Thank You for Your Order*

TOTAL AMOUNT ENCLOSED $_____

**SHIP TO:**

NAME _____

ADDRESS _____

CITY _____ STATE_____ ZIP_____

PHONE(_____) _____ FAX (_____) _____